Hal Arthur

already have ①

# Call to Discipleship

# Call to Discipleship

by
Juan Carlos Ortiz
as told to
Jamie Buckingham

Logos International
Plainfield, New Jersey

Good Reading Limited
London, England

International Standard Book Number: 0–88270–130–4 (cloth)
0–88270–122–3 (paper)
Library of Congress Catalog Card Number: 75–7476
Logos International, Plainfield, New Jersey 07061
Printed in the United States of America

# Editor's Note

This book stems from a series of messages delivered by the author to a conference of pastors in Montreat, North Carolina. He often quoted the traditional Spanish version of the Bible from memory, translating for his hearers as he went. The result is frequently similar to the King James Version, but seldom identical. When this occurs no notation of version is made. At other times he cites various modern English versions which are noted as follows.

RSV, *The Revised Standard Version of the Bible,* © 1946, 1952 by the Division of Christian Education of the National Council of Churches of Christ in the United States of America.

PHILLIPS, *The New Testament in Modern English* translated by J. B. Phillips, © 1957 by the Macmillan Company.

NASB, the *New American Standard Bible,* © 1973 by the Lockman Foundation.

# Publisher's Note

The concept of discipleship is at least as old as the New Testament, but its dramatic reappearance today in the teaching of Juan Carlos Ortiz and others like him have made it seem utterly new to many Christians. And, indeed, much of what he has to say has been neglected by many of us for longer than we might care to admit.

Because the ideas in this book are so fresh and stimulating, we are all in danger of going overboard in our response to them. We will be tempted to try to duplicate what has happened in Argentina by slavish imitation. Let us steadfastly resist such temptation.

When a man becomes a disciple he will learn new vistas of obedience. Discipleship, however, should not finally lead to slavery, but to a deep, mutual bond of friendship. Jesus told his disciples, "No longer do I call you servants . . . but I have called you friends . . . ." (John 15:15). Because we are men we can take truth and twist it just enough to make it serve our own purposes. When this happens, God receives no glory, and our self-serving has an uncanny way of undoing us in the end.

My prayer is that this book, whether you agree or disagree with its contents, will stimulate you to search the scriptures and your hearts anew, and bring you in turn to a deeper commitment to Jesus.

# Contents

# Introduction

Last year a select group of spiritual leaders was invited to Charlotte, North Carolina, to sit under ten hours of intense teaching by Argentine pastor Juan Carlos Ortiz. Even though the teaching was recorded on audio and television tape, there was strong opinion it should not be released to the public.

"Too inflammatory," some thought.

Perhaps they were right, at that time. But God is moving with His own tongues of fire across the world. And the teachings of Juan Carlos are now needed to give additional insight into the move of the Holy Spirit during these last days before the return of Christ.

From the moment this gentle pastor began to teach, I realized I was sitting at the feet of a man who had learned the meaning of the lordship of Jesus Christ. After the manner of the German martyr, Dietrich Bonhoeffer, and the Chinese martyr, Watchman Nee, it was obvious God had also raised up such a man in Latin America—Juan Carlos Ortiz. Like Bonhoeffer and Nee, this articulate teacher has gone far beyond our superficial American concepts of love, lordship, and discipleship to ferret out the real meanings of Jesus' life and teachings.

Ortiz has put his theories into practice in his personal life and his church—with amazing success. In fact, his experiences are not the product of his theories; rather his theories have grown out of the laboratory of experience. During this time "the church of Buenos Aires" has come very close to being a prototype of the New Testament church in the twentieth century.

When Jesus spoke about heaven, people sat up and listened. He was an authority because He had been there. When He spoke about submission to men and obedience to the Father, even the scribes and Pharisees recognized His authority. Why? Because He was what He taught—submissive and obedient.

That was the reason I was forced to listen to this Argentine pastor. He was not just talking theory, he was talking out of personal experience. And even though I cannot agree with all his conclusions, I must listen to them—for he has walked them out.

As I worked over the manuscript of his teachings, I recalled something I had read as a boy—something that had stirred my heart to the deeper things of God. J. B. Phillips had just finished translating the New Testament epistles into modern English. He called it *Letters to Young Churches*. As he struggled with the original text, he said certain spiritual principles became evident to him. He listed them in his "Translator's Preface," then closed by saying:

> It is heartening to remember that this faith took root and flourished amazingly in conditions that would have killed anything less vital in a matter of weeks. These early Christians were on fire with the conviction that they had become, through Christ, literally sons of God; they were pioneers of a new humanity, founders of a new Kingdom. They still speak to us across the

centuries. *Perhaps if we believed what they believed, we might achieve what they achieved.*

Recently a Latin American theologian stated: "The proclamation of the Gospel, apart from the unity of the church, is a theological absurdity." The purpose of the Gospel is to bring people into the church of Jesus Christ— His body. But if that body is split into many different sects and denominations, then it represents, at best, only a portion of the will of God.

In this book Juan Carlos Ortiz gives the basic principles for restoring the Kingdom of God here on earth through the unity of the body. He offers no easy methods. In fact, he offers no methods at all. And even though he translates the principles of Jesus into modern-day application, his conclusions are the same as those presented in the Bible: man must die to self and recognize the lordship of Jesus.

This book is not intended for everyone. It is only for those who are ready to let the Kingdom of God come in their lives, their families, their church.

Many will read these pages and snap shut the doors of their minds just as quickly as they close the book. "Impossible. Too idealistic," they will say knowingly. I am not afraid of these, for we shall always have among us those of limited vision, those afraid to dare.

Others will become angry, for these teachings are so revolutionary that if applied they will literally destroy the comfortable church structures we have built around ourselves. I thank God for those who get angry, for even though this book constitutes a threat to them and their little kingdoms, some will hear the call of Christ and lay down the security of their fishing nets for the walk of faith.

Others will read this book and, too lazy to do their own thinking and praying, will take it and use it as a mechanic's manual, a sort of program plan book for the kingdom. It is these I fear. This is not a book of methods, it is a book of principles. The only way God's methods can be discovered is by using the same principles applied by the author in Argentina:

1. Recognize your need to change.
2. Repent of your old methods and bondage to tradition.
3. Be willing to lose everything for the glory of God.
4. Submit to the lordship of Jesus Christ.
5. Submit to other men of God.
6. Be willing to be used as God's instrument here on earth.
7. When you make mistakes, openly admit them, and start over.
8. Be patient enough to wait five years, or more, before you stand up and proclaim, "This is the way, follow me."

May God deliver us from those who are unwilling to arrive at their own conclusions through prayer, fasting, and waiting on the Lord.

                                        Jamie Buckingham

# Call to Discipleship

# CHAPTER 1

# The Call to Maturity

When I took over the pastoral duties of a Pentecostal church in Buenos Aires, there were 184 members in my flock. The church had been established under the leadership of a missionary, and the denominational headquarters felt that the church was now ready to become self-supporting, assuming the work under a local pastor, as well as assuming financial responsibility. Gone were the days of depending upon their beloved missionary and support from the United States for a piano, literature, and other physical needs.

My wife and I realized at the time that unless there was visible growth in the church, our pastoring days might be of short duration. So we set out to work very hard toward that end—growth. We worked sixteen hours a day, and after two years showed 600 members on the roll. All departments of the church were well organized and functioning. There was a minister of education, men's and women's groups, youth groups, and a follow-up program that covered all possible needs. There were categories 1, 2, 3, for male, female, Arabs, Jews, children, etc. Telephone calls, visitors, subscriptions to helpful magazines—all these were on our agenda of operation. One year we had 3,965 decisions registered in our regular services. These were not from campaigns, just the result of our hard work.

So there I was with a well-oiled piece of machinery on

my hands. But I knew something was wrong. The thing that impressed me was that when I worked hard, everything worked out. When I didn't, the machinery started bogging down. I knew there must be a loose screw somewhere. When I came to this realization, I determined to take time to find out where it was.

It is very difficult for a denominational pastor to stop. How can he explain to his board, "I will stop work for fifteen days to pray"? Perhaps the board will say in return, "Very well, but we are paying you to preach and visit. If you withdraw fifteen days to pray we'll discount those days from your salary."

In Argentina very few people have cars and it's up to the pastor to take everybody to the hospital, take all the women to the doctor when they are going to deliver their children, drive the children to Sunday school . . . in a literal way the pastor is the mover of the congregation. If he is not present, everything grinds to a standstill.

At the same time, I had been so active doing God's business that I had not taken time to ask the Lord if what I was doing was right or wrong, or what it was He wanted me to be doing. I saw that activities were like a wheel: once you got going and momentum increased, it was very difficult to stop long enough to get off.

Before breakfast the phone began ringing—and so it went far into the night. There was some time for study, for writing sermons, and for some personal devotions, but there was never time to wait on the Lord for His word to us. There were monthly newsletters on how to do things, but no time for letters to the churches from the Holy Spirit. I thought what we were doing was right because it came from the central office, but now I wanted to find out for myself. I made a decision to set aside one week and I went out in the country, away from all the activity, to seek the Lord.

While I was there God spoke to me very clearly. "Juan, where is My finger in all this? You are dealing with My things—and you are promoting them as Coca-Cola promotes its product, as *Reader's Digest* sells records and books. The letters, the visits, the phone calls—but where is My finger?"

In the face of that probing question there was only one reply I could make. "Lord, I don't see Your finger anywhere. I am applying everything I learned at school and in seminars, but there is no moving of Your spirit."

Following that admission, God began speaking to me about the condition of the church. He said that we were not growing. My reply to that was, "Lord, we *are* growing. We have gone from 200 to 600 in two years."

Then came this even more startling revelation. "You are not growing; you are just getting fat. You just have more people of the same kind. You had 200 without love, then 300, 500, now 600—all without love. More of the same . . . not growing . . . getting fat." And I had to admit this was true. I had never sought growth in my congregation, just additions. We had only multiplied more babes.

God went even further: "Yours is not a church; it is an orphanage. No one there has a parent; all are orphans and you are the director of the orphanage. Sundays you fill a bottle of milk and say, 'Now open your mouths.' And you think you are feeding your people."

This presented a crisis and I did not know what to do about it. But God, in His mercy, made a move toward His solution. A group of pastors in our city began coming together. At first the group was called the Charismatic

Group. The basis of unity was the experience of the baptism of the Spirit and operation of the charismata—the gifts of the Spirit. But after a while, we learned that this was a wrong basis for unity. We could see that even denominations centered on this experience were divided and that no one experience or doctrine can be an acceptable center for God's unity. We came to understand that the unity of the church is based on the lordship of Jesus Christ, His love, and the fruit of the Spirit.

Once we accepted this center for our fellowship, we found ourselves sharing and receiving from each other. I was asked to teach about the charismata, and as I taught, I realized many there had something our church lacked— love. I resolved to take this need back to my people. I was also able to share with the group of ministers what God had told me about getting fat, about orphans and milk. Soon God began to give us answers to these and other questions that came out of our sharing. Throughout the next five years God moved in a very wonderful way in our midst.

## The Eternal Childhood of the Believer

As I understand it, the church of today faces three basic problems. The first is the eternal childhood of the believer. The second is the misplacement of the believer. The third is the lack of unity. This became evident when I surveyed my own situation in our church. Although we were adding more and more people to the membership roll, all were remaining children, little babes who had to be taught the same things year after year.

The hymns we sang, the prayers we prayed, told us that we were only children. Not only were we content to use the same hymns and prayers for forty years, but they were always on the same subject: asking. Yet I knew that when a child grows, the clothes don't fit him any more.

In our situation we had been using the same hymn book for over forty years. Now, since God has renewed us, we've changed the hymn book five times in five years. It is the same way with our prayers. If after ten years of going to church you hear the same prayers by the same people, you know the church has not grown. We are commanded to grow in prayer, praise, worship, ministry, and singing.

Suppose I were to go home after a trip and speak to my wife the same way I spoke to her twelve years ago when she was among a group of girls in my congregation.

"Sister Martha, if we can be alone, I would like to speak a few words, please."

"Certainly, pastor. Let's go and speak together."

"Sister Martha, I don't know if you have noticed or not, but I feel something different for you from what I feel for the other sisters in the congregation."

"Why no, pastor, I had not noticed" (blush, blush!).

What a strange conversation for a couple who have been married twelve years and have four children!

No, because we have been together for a long time, and have been intimate all that time, my conversation has changed. I no longer call her Sister Martha. I call her Darling. I now tell her everything because we have grown in fellowship. We've grown in dialogue. We've grown in knowing each other.

People who sing the same hymns for years, pray the same prayers for years, keep the same church structure, and need the same messages are not really growing. They are eternal children.

Paul told the Corinthians they were babes because they were divided. But the division Paul accuses them of is not the division we have today. All the Corinthians were in the same church, only they were divided over their leaders. Some said that Paul was the founder of the church so they should follow him. Others said Peter was better because he had been with Jesus. Still others were thrilled with the preaching of Apollos. "When Apollos preaches even the benches tremble," they said. All in the same church, yet divided over their preachers.

For this, Paul called them babes. If this is what it is to be babes, what would Paul call us today? Today we have pastors who won't even talk to one another. The churches are all divided into different buildings in different places speaking against one another and calling themselves by different names. If the Corinthians were babes, we are not even born yet. And it continues. Instead of becoming one, we are dividing more and more each day. Different denominations start. Today the body of Christ is divided as never before in history. We are less than babes.

Our childishness is shown in our prayers. "Heal me, help me, baptize me, prosper me, me, me." The "me" center, the "I" center, is childhood. Children are always asking, "Give me, Daddy, give me, Mommy. Give me a dollar. Give me some ice cream. Give me this. Give me that." Only a mature person knows how to give. As a little babe I was continually asking. Now I am continually giving. Why? Because I am now mature. I have grown, so I must give and give and give.

Children are always seeking for gifts—more than for fruit. If a healer or evangelist comes to our church, you'll see in the crowd those who never come to the regular meetings. The children all turn out to see the spectacular gifts, much as children love to go to magic shows. But only the mature people will seek the fruit of the Spirit: love, joy, peace, longsuffering, etc.

Materialism is also an evidence of childhood. Children do not know how to value things. Perhaps a child has a hundred-dollar bill in his hand, but you show him a chocolate bar and he'll leave the hundred-dollar bill for the chocolate. Church members demonstrate their childishness by their craving for material things—good homes, good cars, money—while they leave spiritual things in second place. Eternal childhood.

Our lack of workers is additional evidence of our eternal childhood. I don't know how it can be, but there are people who spend ten, twenty years in church and still do not know how to lead a person to Christ. The only thing they can do is invite them to a meeting. They say to a friend, "Why don't you come to our church? It has comfortable benches, new carpeting, heat in winter and air conditioning in summer. We have a nice preacher too. Why don't you come?"

Twenty years to learn to invite a person to a meeting! Then it is up to the pastor to lead those souls to Christ, feed them the milk of the Word, and baptize them. Paul almost never baptized anybody in Corinth. He said, "I don't think I ever baptized any of you. Oh yes, I think I baptized Crispus and Gaius."

If you read the Acts you find that Crispus was the first that God saved at Corinth and Gaius was the second. It seems that Paul baptized the first two—Crispus and Gaius—and they baptized the others. Why? Because Paul was making disciples. He was not fattening the church, he was letting it multiply.

But in our churches pastors are always doing the same thing because people do not grow. We pastors are continually preaching the ABCs of the gospel. Every Sunday people come to the altar. We put them in the classes for new people, give them lessons on the church, and baptism—then we start with another group. But while we are starting with another group, these first people are getting lost because we didn't take them into maturity. We are like doctors bringing children into the world. But many of our children die because we don't take them on to maturity. We gain so many people each year, and we lose so many people. Almost all churches are winning people but few that are won stay in the church. We cannot raise them up in the church because we have eternal children.

Who is guilty in this situation? Many times we say to the people, "You are babes, you must grow." But a person who is fed only on milk cannot grow. The pastors are guilty because they are always giving them milk. But how can you blame the pastor when he has been taught this by his seminary and denominational leaders? The only way out is to stop all activities and ask God if we are doing the right thing or not.

Bound in activities, I found myself on a wheel that couldn't stop. Telephone calls in the morning, interviews, Bible studies, commitments here and there to preach, and I could never stop. So I taught things as they came from the Bible schools, from the Sunday school materials. I received materials from the central office and put them into practice without even asking God about them. We had a Women's Society because that is how we were taught from the central office. We had the Young People's Association because that is how we were taught from the central office. Everything we did was because it came from the central office. We never stopped to ask the Lord if this was from Him or not. And I doubt if the central office of the denomination ever stopped to ask either. They were as active as we. Nobody stopped. We just kept going, doing the same things for years, never stopping to ask God if what we were doing was His will or not.

Of course the denomination was proud of me. I was called to be the main speaker in two conventions to share my follow-up system with them. I gave each pastor a sample of all the papers we had, all kinds of papers and letters. Then God told me His finger was not in all those things and in desperation I withdrew to try to hear from God.

Studying the epistle to the Hebrews, I came to chapter six, which I had never understood clearly. This time, however, a small light illuminated it. Here the author speaks of "leaving the principles of the doctrine of Christ (repentance, faith, baptism, baptism in the Holy Spirit, eternal judgment) and going on unto perfection." I could not imagine what it meant to leave these things and go forward. After all, those things comprised all my teaching and doctrine.

I examined all my sermons and Bible studies for the previous twenty years. As I suspected, they were all on repentance, faith in God, baptism in water, baptism in the Holy Spirit, the second coming of Christ with the resurrection of the dead and the final judgment. All my sermons and studies were upon the themes that the scripture called "rudiments."

When I read the Sunday school material that came

for the five-year terms, I discovered that all our teaching was based on the first principles of the gospel. When I read over all the materials I had in seminary, I found out that in seminary we were taught only the first principles of the gospel. On the shelves in my study I had many books on Systematic Theology. Invariably, though, the chapters of these books were titled:

    I. The Holy Scripture
   II. God
  III. Man
  IV. Salvation
   V. Jesus Christ
  VI. The Second Coming
 VII. Last Things.

That's all I had in my books. But those were just the first principles of the oracles of God.

I belonged to a church that was proud to preach four main things: salvation, baptism in the Holy Spirit, healing, and the second coming of Christ. And my church called this the *Full Gospel.* But now I discovered that those things we called the Full Gospel weren't even first principles.

Many other congregations had this same problem. If we say "emptiness" is "full," how can we grow? I thought I had everything when I really had pitifully little.

Not long ago I met a pastor from another denomination. He asked me, "Are you Brother Ortiz?"

I said yes.

He said, "I am getting into deep water. I am learning of another dimension of the Gospel that I never thought of before. Brother, I am speaking in tongues."

He thought he had arrived at the climax of experience when Paul didn't even list tongues as milk. It was one of the first principles. All the things we were preaching continually month after month, year after year—repentance, faith, baptism—were the ABCs. That was the reason the people had not grown.

A boy in my congregation who had been saved before the renewal started said, "Within six months of my conversion I knew everything everybody else knew in the church. From that six months on, I was just maintained in the congregation. I grew just so far and I stayed there."

You see, people get bored with church. It's not that Satan tempts them, it's because we are always in the same first principles of the Gospel.

Paul speaks of solid food. He tells the Corinthians that he cannot give them solid food yet because they are still babes. To the Hebrews he says "let us go on to maturity." I think, however, that much of the letter to the Hebrews is still in the realm of elementary doctrine. Romans is based on first principles. Romans speaks of developed salvation. In our seminary, however, Hebrews and Romans were the epistles for the third year. They were so deep. But when we revisit them we find out they are explanations of the first principles of salvation. So where, and what, is the solid food?

After speaking to the Corinthian children of the rudiments (the message of Christ crucified), Paul says, "Howbeit we speak wisdom among them that are perfect" (I Cor. 2:6). Paul thus indicates why he spoke only of Christ crucified. It did not signify that this was the entire message of God's salvation. But he did indicate this was only the beginning, the entrance—a rudiment. He explains that those who have reached maturity should not speak the wisdom of this age, but things which eye has not seen nor ear heard, that which *God has revealed to the mature.*

Then he says that in spite of all these revelations for those who have reached maturity, they, the Corinthians, cannot receive them because they are still children and therefore must continue drinking milk. From this we deduce that the entire epistle to the Corinthians is light milk for children. That includes Paul's teachings on immorality, lawsuits before unconverted persons, matrimonial problems, food sacrificed to idols, insubordination, women's dress, idolatry, abuses in the Lord's Supper, spiritual gifts (especially tongues), the resurrection of the dead, and offerings—all are milk for children.

Additional insight is found in the following verses:

> But as it is written, Eye hath not seen, nor ear heard, neither have entered into the heart of man, the things which God hath prepared for them that love him. But God hath revealed them unto us by his Spirit: for the Spirit searcheth all things, yea, the deep things of God. For what man knoweth the things of a man, save the spirit of man which is in him? even so the things of God knoweth no man, but the Spirit of God. Now we have received, not the spirit of the world, but the spirit which is of God; that we might know the things that are freely given to us of God. Which things also we speak, not in the words which man's wisdom teacheth, but which the Holy Ghost teacheth; comparing spiritual things with spiritual. But the natural man receiveth not the things of the Spirit of God: for they are foolishness unto him: neither can he know them, because they are spiritually discerned. But he that is spiritual judgeth all things, yet he himself is judged by no man. For who hath known the mind of the Lord, that he may instruct him? But we have the mind of Christ (I Corinthians 2:9–16).

You see, to receive solid food, somebody must go

behind the curtain. If we spend all our time with the ABCs of the gospel, we will never get into the holiest where the "mystery, the hidden wisdom" is to be found.

I was concerned because I realized I was so busy preaching salvation, inviting men to come to the altar, playing the organ, and bringing in new babes that there was no time left to lead the new converts on to maturity. I left them at the altar and busied myself in bringing in more orphans. I knew that to carry the believers of my church on to maturity, I first had to begin growing myself.

In his letter to the church at Ephesus (the most "grown-up" church of all those founded by Paul), he wrote, "I pray to God that he may give you the spirit of wisdom and of revelation to *a knowledge of himself*" (Eph. 1:17). Paul knew what was to be gained through a spirit of revelation. God had taken him to the third heaven and revealed to him part of this knowledge "of Himself." Exactly how much, we do not know; but we do know that of all God revealed to him, he was allowed to tell only a part (see II Corinthians 12 for Paul's words on his experiences). Not only could Paul tell only a portion of what he knew; but of all that he did teach, we have only a part which is recorded in his letters. And many of his writings were not in the "mainstream" of what he taught, but were written to "correct" the teachings he had already given them when he was with them in person. Thus, of all the principles we have preserved for us, we understand very little—and we practice very little of what we do understand. Yet if Paul, in that beginning of the church, could have such a vision, such a revelation, how much more should we who live in the end time when the church should be in its final stages of growth.

# CHAPTER 2

# From Milk to Meat

Why did Jesus put ministers in the church?

And he gave some apostles; and some prophets; and some evangelists; and some pastors and teachers; For the perfecting (maturing) of the saints, for the work of the ministry, for the edifying of the body of Christ (Eph. 4:11–12).

Herein lies part of the answer. The purpose of the preaching and teaching in the church is to perfect (bring to maturity) the saints for the work of the ministry. The one learning today is to become a teacher tomorrow. The pastors are not to *entertain* or *maintain* the believers, but to mature them. In other words, shepherds are not placed in the flock to give milk to the sheep. God provides milk to every mother to give her child. Ministers must take the sheep into maturity.

God gave the church ministers to equip and perfect the saints. Yet most of the activities we have in the church are to maintain the saints rather than equip them.

When I go off and visit a church I am often asked by the pastor, "Brother Juan, have you any new idea for the businessmen's association of the church? Have you any new idea for the young people? Our women's organization is dying, can you give me an idea on how to bring it back to life?"

But that's not our ministry. Our ministry is to equip them, to perfect them, to make out of them teachers that they may teach others. That meant I as a pastor needed to have a clear vision of the objective of my existence. What does God wish me to make of the believers? Each pastor must ask himself, "Why did God put me in the ministry? What is my work? To what should I dedicate myself?" The answer to this question is always, "To perfect the saints for the work of the ministry, that Christians might be properly equipped for their service" (PHILLIPS).

How then are we supposed to go about leading the people from being milk-drinkers to being meat-eaters? Paul tells the Hebrews they should already have been teachers, which means that the Christian is really progressing when he can teach and guide someone else to be a Christian. "For though by this time you ought to be teachers, you need someone to teach you again" (Heb. 5:12 RSV). Phillips, translating the same passage, says, "At a time when you should be teaching others, you need teachers yourselves to repeat to you the ABCs of God's revelation to men." This means we should graduate sometime, for if we do not advance we are slipping back. We should pass from the first grade of the rudiments to the second grade of the pure milk, and on to the third grade of solid food.

When I read what Paul said, that he was working to present every man perfect (mature) in Jesus Christ, I cried out, "I am ashamed to present my church to Jesus Christ—all these babes, crying, fussing, criticizing." I would have to admonish them, "Please, children, behave properly, for Jesus is coming; let Him at least see a little bit of order."

I could hear Jesus saying to me, "Juan, I did not put you here to be a baby-sitter." I began to see that there must be purpose in activity. I was to challenge my members to change—to conform to the image of Jesus Christ. These are my disciples and I am to perfect them for the work of the ministry.

What is the work of the ministry? The sheep must multiply themselves. Pastors do not bring forth sheep, the sheep must do it. How can they do this if they are fed only milk? The ministers are not to do all the work of the ministry, but to train the saints, to equip the saints, that they may do the work of the ministry. It is not the architect or the engineer who constructs the building; the engineers and the architects show others how to make the building. The architect can do many buildings at the same time. If the architect would have to take the bricks and make the building himself, he probably couldn't do more than one building in all his life. We need apostolic ministry. We need people who know the "how-to" and the blueprint of God for the church today, to equip the saints for the ministry.

So, the saints are those who must do the work of the ministry. It means that we ministers do not have to bring forth sheep. The sheep must bring forth sheep. Not only are they to bring forth sheep, they also must feed the sheep with milk. Milk is given by the same sheep that gives them birth. Cows produce calves, fig trees produce figs, and sheep produce lambs. Therefore, ministers must produce ministers. So the sheep multiply and feed their young with their own milk, and we ministers take those sheep and make ministers out of them.

This is what we call multiplication. Our classical

evangelism system is not multiplication, however. If I want to be multiplied by ten, it is not because I want ten new souls for the Lord Jesus. Rather I want ten Juan Carlos Ortizes—ten like me. Multiplication involves quality also, not only numbers. If you have an orange and you want to multiply it into ten, it's because you want ten oranges, not ten stems, or ten leaves. Jesus multiplied Himself by twelve, but by twelve like Himself. The twelve apostles were to be as much like Jesus Christ as possible. This is what Paul means when he says we are to equip the saints for the work of the ministry.

We should try to make everybody around us our disciples according to the image of Jesus Christ. The Father's will is to have a family of children like Jesus Christ. But you cannot make others in the image of Jesus Christ if you are not made first. So the first goal in life is to be like Jesus. That means maturity. Paul also says in this same chapter, Ephesians 4, that we must not be any longer children tossed here and there by every wind of doctrine. We are to grow until we attain the unity of the faith and the knowledge of the Son of God—to the measure of the stature which belongs to the fullness of Christ. That's our goal. I must be like Christ, and those around me must follow, that through me they may become like Christ too.

It matters not whether we believe this perfection is absolute or relative, because Christ Himself is the measure of perfection, and our ministry is to make the believers into the image of Christ, bring them to the full stature of Christ, to a perfect man. That is the unequivocal goal of the minister. It is not a question of discussing whether I can reach it or not. I must aim at a target from the very first day I begin to learn to shoot. It is not a question of saying, "It is impossible to hit the target, therefore I will aim anywhere I please." Many say, "We will never reach perfection." They don't have any goal, and so they live mediocre lives. We must lead our believers toward perfection, until Christ shall be formed in them. His character, His love, His grace. That is the target.

But the task is not simply "the perfecting of the saints," but "the perfecting of the saints *for the work of the ministry*."

Not all is accomplished when a believer becomes like Christ in character. He must also be like Him in service. We must develop in them the priesthood and the apostleship, even as Christ is our high priest and apostle. The shepherds do not beget sheep. The sheep reproduce themselves. Nor does the shepherd give milk to the sheep. The sheep nourish each other. The shepherd merely leads the sheep to green pastures. The believers must be able to give birth to other believers and then teach them the rudiments.

In this way, the entire church is comprised of ministers. The ministers are not a special breed of sheep coming from the seminary. They are simply believers who go on growing. Thus the purpose of the pastor is to make disciples who make disciples who make disciples who make disciples.

Paul died in peace because he knew men like Timothy, Philemon, Titus, and Epaphras were carrying on his work. Jesus Himself went to heaven with inner peace because He left a congregation that did not need to write a mission board and say, "Please, send us another pastor because our pastor went up in a cloud to heaven." No, when Jesus went to heaven He left eleven men, eleven men like Himself. Men equipped to minister to the saints.

God has only one agency on this earth, the church. Other agencies apart from the church are not the ultimate will of God. I am not against seminaries and Bible schools. I am glad we have them. But we cannot be satisfied with building factories to make crutches. It would be better to look for the healing of the church. Once the church gets healed, the crutches will fall away. It is dangerous to yank crutches away from people. However, once they are healed, the crutches will be left behind. Our task is to serve God and pray that He quickly heals His church.

# CHAPTER 3

# Mandate to Grow

When I got serious with God and began to pray, "Lord, I want to feed your sheep, I want to give them solid food," I discovered some principles I had never seen before. For instance, Paul told the Corinthian church that "God has appointed in the church first apostles, second prophets, third teachers, then workers of miracles, then healers, helpers, administrators, speakers in various kinds of tongues" (1 Cor. 12:28, rsv).

I had never paid any attention to what he meant by "first, second, and third," because I knew nothing about growing. I thought I had the full gospel: salvation, healing, tongues, and the second coming of the Lord. I thought a grown-up person was one who knew about repentance, faith, and the baptism in the Holy Spirit. Then I began to discover the principles of growth.

The first principle I saw was that apostleship is really a ministry that includes all the other ministries. An apostle was a prophet, teacher, and worker of miracles. He could heal, help, administer, and speak in tongues. It was interesting to discover that the element I had always considered to be the diploma (tongues) was really the starting point. In the New Testament people often spoke in tongues the day they got converted.

Now, where was our church on this list? We were in tongues, and not well spoken at that. I believe in tongues, although I think many people have made it just another "me" ministry instead of bringing glory to God. However, any way you look at it, tongues is just the starting point.

If I have a hundred persons in my church who speak in tongues this year, and next year I have three hundred tongues speakers, and the following year four hundred— I'm not growing. I'm just getting fat. I have more people of the same kind. You have a hundred people this year without love, next year two hundred without love, then four hundred without love, then a thousand without love—you are just getting fat. You have a hundred babes, then two hundred babes, then five hundred babes—but always babes. Most families grow naturally. Usually when the second child comes, the first one is, perhaps, three years old. The problem in the church is the second one comes while the first one is still a baby. Then we add a third and all three are babes. Seldom do we see one grow up.

Look at the example of Paul's life. Paul was not an apostle from the beginning. In the beginning he was just a disciple who witnessed to the churches. First he witnessed. Then he spoke in tongues. Next he became an administrator. He was a help to Barnabas. He healed. He performed miracles. He made some mistakes. He later became a teacher in Antioch. He was among the prophets. Finally he was sent forth as an apostle.

But in our modern ministries the situation is different. Some know how to speak in tongues, others how to administrate, others how to help, and others how to perform healings. But most don't grow. Our church structure doesn't allow it. People get saved and they start to grow. They hear the sermons, the teaching, until they reach the spiritual level of the pastor—and stop. And the church becomes a chamber of tensions.

The pastor is the cork in the church. Nobody can go out because the pastor is not perfecting the saints for the work of the ministry. Rather, he is preventing the saints from becoming ministers. It isn't that he doesn't want his people to grow; rather, there is no room in the church structure for growth. To see the answer we have to go back to Jesus. Jesus was not a pastor of the church. He had no desire to establish a big congregation because he had no ego that had to be fed. He left this earth in order that his disciples might grow and move along in their church.

When I leave my church in Argentina for a trip abroad I often receive letters from my disciples. "Every time you leave, we weep. But when you are out we understand how much we need to stay alone." That's part of teaching—to leave them alone in the congregation. Disciples who four years ago couldn't even pray out loud are now pastors of the church. This sets me free to travel up to eight months of the year. This is good since my constant presence would make me a cork in the local church. When I am present nobody else will preach, and the sheep all come flocking to me instead of to the other pastors. Therefore I stay on the move to keep from becoming a cork.

Denominational thinking leads to a different solution. The pastor tells the bishop the problems he has with the deacons. The bishop removes the pastor from the church and puts him in another church. He then brings in another cork to tell them the same thing in different words. So you see, changing pastors every other year does not solve the problem—for the cork remains, only with another name.

But in the congregational church, where there is no bishop, the problem is worse. Here the tensions become so great that suddenly the cork explodes. Boom! And the pastor flies out. Poor pastor! Sometimes when one of these pastors is kicked out, he cannot be a pastor any more because the people have said so many things against him. But if the pastor grows and takes his people with him as he grows, the church remains happy and tranquil.

Now a club can change presidents each year by election. But a church should never change pastors because it is a family, and the pastor should be the father. Whoever heard of a family that changed fathers every other year, or of a father who ran off and left his family to take on another larger family? The father should be training his sons to take over the business. Thus it stands to reason that any young man wanting to learn about the kingdom would turn to his pastor for instruction. Instead he leaves the church to go to Bible School, because the church is failing in its commission.

When I was twenty years old I was founding churches—not real churches, just corner stores. Had there been an apostle in my boyhood church who was making disciples I would have gone out and established real churches—factories. But as a lamb I led my people to feed on me, as though I were the green pasture (when in truth I was only a *green pastor*). Thus when I went out I had to enlist another green pastor to come in and run my fruit stand. In a factory I would have developed many pastors to replace me.

Paul went out and made factory churches. He taught people. He made disciples. When he left a place, the church stayed there. After two years he said, "Barnabas, let's go visit the brethren to see how they are." When they went back the brethren were still there. And not only still there, but the church was growing. Paul's disciples worked so much that when he went to the next province he didn't need to talk because his disciples had already gone before him.

Only an apostle makes factory churches. Others make fruit stands.

When the scattered and persecuted believers got to Antioch they started a church. After several years Barnabas and Paul arrived also. Soon they were numbered among the other prophets and teachers. Of course there were miracles, healings, helps, and administration. But when it was time to send out workers, who went? The Spirit didn't say, "Set apart for the work of the ministry that nice boy who plays the accordion so well." No, He said, "Set apart the principals, Saul and Barnabas."

Today it's all upside down. We expect the pastor to be in the pulpit each Sunday. "Oh, no one can feed me like my green pasture," we sigh, not realizing he is a cork in the neck of the bottle.

In the primitive church the most successful pastor was the one who could make the children grow faster and better until they took over his job—freeing him to go out and establish other church families. He could leave the church in the children's hands. Paul could always come to his home in Antioch. He went out and he came back. But he was always making factories as a true apostle always does.

The Greek word behind our word apostle is the same as the Latin term behind our word missionary. But that doesn't mean everyone we call a missionary is necessarily an apostle. Flying down to Argentina in a plane to pastor a church does not make an American a missionary, no matter how many mission boards lay hands on him. An Argentine pastor can do the same job for only $100 per month where an American needs much more than that just to live up to his usual standard. How wasteful. How expensive. No, an apostle is one who establishes and makes workers. Many missionaries have come to Argentina as pastors of small churches. How much better to train leaders, and then leave. That is the commission of Jesus. Go, and make disciples.

The pattern of Paul's ministry is found in I Thessalonians 1:6–9.

> You also became imitators of us, and of the Lord, having received the word in much tribulation with the joy of the Holy Spirit, so that you became an example to all the believers in Macedonia and Achaia. For the word of the Lord has sounded forth from you, not only in Macedonia and Achaia, but also in every place your faith toward God has gone forth, so that we have no need to say anything. For they themselves report about us what kind of a reception we had with you, and how you turned to God from idols to serve a living and true God. . . . (NASB)

What a church! The sheep matured to the point where they, in turn, could teach others who would serve as examples of their teachings everywhere they went.

# CHAPTER 4

# The Misplacement of the Believer

Each believer needs to know his place in the body. Most church congregations are not a spiritual building, but a mountain of bricks. There is a difference. However good the materials may be, if they are not situated in their right place and correctly related to one another, there is no building. Each member of the congregation is a brick. The evangelists are continually bringing in new bricks. The pastor encourages this, even teaching classes on soul-winning. Bring in more bricks, he urges. But bricks are not a building. Instead of a builder, the pastor now becomes a caretaker of bricks.

The problem of having a mountain of bricks on the land is that when the bricks are not built into a building they can be stolen or broken up. Therefore the pastor is continually having to take care of the bricks, because some other pastor or Satan might steal them. But the Bible tells us pastors are for edifying the body of Christ, not just for caretaking of bricks. Our churches are like mountains of members; they have hands, legs, ears, and noses, but they are not a body. They are not a building, just a mountain of bricks.

So, why is it that nobody knows his place? It's because the pastors are not fulfilling their duty. They are just bringing in the bricks—making campaigns, having evangelistic meetings, giving out tracts, growing numerically. Bricks. Bricks. Instead of taking each brick to be a part of a building, he's just taking care of them. But in God's temple, each person must know which brick is under him, which brick is beside him, and which brick is going to be over him. He must be in his place. Jesus said He put pastors in the church, not to bring in more bricks, but to build His temple.

One of the reasons for this trouble is the structure of the congregation—pastor and laymen, the director of the orphanage and the orphans. In both Catholic and evangelical churches there is a marked difference between "clergy" and "laity." In this classical relationship the believers pay a salary to the pastor who in turn offers his services—preaching, visiting, performing ceremonies, and organizing committees. In many congregations the believers elect their pastor and the deacons, unless he is an especially vigorous leader, tell him what to do. If the pastor and deacons disagree, the deacons usually have the last word.

But the pastor-laymen concept is not biblical. God wants to have a kingdom of priests. We are all priests. Martin Luther discovered that all believers are priests. Praise the Lord, that was a very good discovery. Now, God is calling us to function as such. If we are all priests, then the laymen must be those who are not saved, those to whom we should minister. But we are so occupied with all our babes that the needy ones never receive our time.

Another reason for misplacement of the believer is the democratic concept. People don't want to submit to anybody. They say proudly, "I don't follow any man. I follow Christ." That sounds nice, but it is really a great mistake. He really means, "I want to do my own will." He doesn't believe that to follow Christ means submitting to other Christians. Paul says, "Be followers of me. Be imitators of me as I am an imitator of Christ." But as a preacher I was continually saying, with great piosity, "Don't look to me, brothers. Don't look at man. Look at the Bible." What that means is, "I looked at the Bible but could not find the truth for you. Now you must try." But Paul accepted the challenge. He said, "Be ye imitators of me."

The believer is misplaced because the church uses a system of addition instead of the system of multiplication. Once an old woman in my country introduced me to a tall girl. She said, "This is my granddaughter."

I said, "Have you really a granddaughter as old as this?"

"Oh," she said, "I have great-grandchildren. One great-granddaughter is fifteen. If she gets married soon, I'll have great-great-grandchildren."

"How many children did you have?" I asked.

She replied, "I had six!"

"And how many grandsons?"

"Thirty-six."

"And how many great-grandchildren?"

"I don't know," she said, "who knows?"

According to this proportion she could have 216 great-grandchildren, and 1,296 great-great-grandchildren. What a big church—for only one woman! But this is not all. She has one son who is a doctor and one a lawyer. Two are pharmacists, another is a taxicab driver. Then among the grandsons there are engineers and every other kind of profession. And all of these are studying.

"How can you care for so many?" I asked. "How did they all get fed, clothed, and educated?"

"Oh," she said, "I only took care of these six. And each one of them took care of their six." This is the system of multiplication over against the system of addition.

Another cause for the misplacement of believers is the Sunday school. The early church knew nothing about Sunday schools. They knew the best way for believers to grow and multiply is not through Bible lectures, but through living cells. This means small groups of four or five persons who meet in homes under a leader so their lives may be shaped so they may mobilize and multiply themselves in other cells. If all contact with the believers is through the official services of the church and the sporadic visits of pastors without dedicating time to place each one of his proper sphere of work, guiding him, controlling him, assigning him specific tasks and correcting the results, the believers will continually remain misplaced.

How can these problems be solved? Paul says God established pastors ". . . for the edifying of the body of Christ" (Eph. 2:21). "To edify" means to build. This means making disciples out of the people. Everyone who comes into the church is one more brick piling up in the place of worship. The work of the pastor is not that of a watchman who takes care that no one robs the bricks as they keep piling up, but of a stone mason who builds them into the edifice. Sadly, though, the work of many pastors is nothing more than bringing bricks and taking care that they are not stolen—like a night watchman in a brickyard.

Nevertheless, Paul tells us that the minister was not called for this but to *edify,* to put every "living stone" in its

place and to make of them "a holy temple unto the Lord."
This word edify, to build, to construct a building, must be
graven upon our hearts as a plumbline for our motives. All
those church members must be perfected for the work of
the ministry and made into a building. Every one is a
"living stone," not dead, and the building is one that
"grows into a holy temple in the Lord." Someone steals
one brick from the pile of materials, perhaps it will not be
noticed. But if someone robs a brick that has been placed
in the building, it will leave a hole. Fortunately, however, a
brick that has been cemented into a building and is
surrounded by (related to) other bricks, is hard to pry
loose. To get it you have to attack the entire building.

A building is more than one person. Perhaps you are
the foreman, but above you are expert architects and
under you are masons and other workmen, but the
important thing is the building where all the members are
well placed. Of course we are not building just a common
structure, but the body of Christ. Much of the work done
in conventions, regional gatherings, and committees is for
the purpose of consolidating and aggrandizing the denomination more than the body of Christ. Thus much work is
duplicated. Printing presses, publishing houses, buildings,
retirement homes, costly sanctuaries—many in the same
city. Thus we must ponder what we are building, whether
it is a separate kingdom or whether it is really the body of
Christ, where one member is joined with another member
as in the human body.

Jesus was the best pastor. Nevertheless, when He saw
the multitudes who were listening to Him, He said, "I see
the multitudes as sheep without a pastor." Was He not a
pastor of a big church? Had He not twelve deacons? But

He saw the people without a shepherd. What did He mean? He meant that a pastor is not to have a flock of one hundred or two hundred. Each pastor should be a father who will raise children who in turn will be fathers and raise children. If Jesus didn't make more than twelve disciples, how can I make five hundred? He Himself took just twelve and taught them very well, and told those twelve afterwards, "You go now and make disciples. Do the same thing I did with you." That is the only way the bricks can become a building, the members a body.

Instead of teaching people in small families, in small cells, in small homes as in the early church, however, we enjoy the big crowds. A thousand come on Sunday and we say, "Come on, open your mouths! Well—you are fed. Goodbye. You are dismissed." That's not the way to feed children. We must take them one by one, put the bottle in their mouths, and train them to move on to meat so they can grow sufficiently to feed others.

Jesus understood that. That is the reason why, even though He was present, He said the sheep were without a pastor. And He chose the twelve to be the pastors. And those twelve made pastors of others. That is the plan of God.

If we do not discern the body of Christ, we are guilty of the body and of the blood of Christ, Paul says. To discern the body of Christ is to understand that we are one. If you do not understand what the body of Christ is, you cannot edify the body of Christ. Perhaps one day I see a man who is cutting his foot. I say, "What are you doing?"

"I'm cutting my foot."

"Why?"

"Because this foot is hurting the other one, and he said, 'Cut it!'"

That is crazy. Only an insane person would not have the discernment that this foot belonged to the body.

Many times, when I am teaching, I accidentally bite my tongue. But I never consider taking all my teeth out! Because the tongue, even when he can speak, doesn't say, "Pull all the teeth out." He understands that the teeth belong to the body.

I have very rebellious hair. But I love it, I take care of it. When I see that it is falling, I look for lotions to put on it. Why? Because I don't want to lose it. I understand my body.

Even so, we must discern the body of Christ. We must understand what the body of Christ is. If you see a person hurting himself, it is because he is insane. Only insane people do that! The church then, must be insane! When one church speaks against the others, when one denomination fights with the others, we are hurting our own body. That is the reason we are so weak and blinded.

Those who killed the physical body of Christ, those who shed His blood, at least had a purpose. What purpose is there, today, in crucifying and hurting and dividing this body of Christ? There is no purpose. So the punishment of those who hurt and bleed this body of Christ, the church, is going to be much greater than the punishment of those who crucified the physical body of Jesus Christ. This is what Paul means—that one who drinks without discernment, without knowing what is the body of Christ—is going to be guilty of the blood and of the body of Jesus Christ.

When you drink your next glass of water, know that

He is the water of life too. When you take a piece of bread for lunch, ask God to reveal to you the body of Christ. If we don't build the body of Christ, if we don't bring the entire church into unity, we are not really ministers of Jesus Christ, because ministers of Jesus Christ are for the edifying of the body of Christ. God give us a vision of the body of Christ.

CHAPTER 5

# The Duty of a Servant

## Who Is a Servant?

A slave or a servant in the days of Jesus was a person who had lost everything in this world. He had lost his liberty, his will, even his name. Perhaps he was a person of worth until he was sold in the market like an animal. In the market a price was put on his neck and people bargained for him. When the slave was taken home, a hole was made in his ear and a ring put in with the name of the owner on it. The slaves even lost their own names. They were not called John or Peter any more, but the slave of Mr. Smith, the slave of Mr. Williams. A slave had lost every freedom. He was not paid for the work he did; he was the property of the owner. He had to work from morning to night. If the owner said, "You must get up at six," he had to get up at six. If the owner wanted him to get up and work at midnight, he had to do it. He had no choice; he was bought with a price. The owner had all power over him. He had nothing to say but only to obey.

Now along comes Jesus who says to His disciples, "Which of you, having a slave plowing or tending sheep, will say to him when he has come in from the field, 'Come immediately and sit down to eat.'" And the disciples laughed. Nobody, if he owns a slave. For the slave has first to serve the master. Only then, when the master was satisfied and went to bed, could a slave sit and eat the things left from the master's dinner. That was the law.

Jesus continued, "But he will say to him, 'Prepare something for me to eat and properly clothe yourself and serve me until I have eaten and drunk and afterward you will eat and drink.' "

The disciples said, "Yes, of course."

"The master did not thank the slave because he did the things which were commanded, did he?"

"Of course not," said the disciples. "But what has this thing to do with us?"

"So you too. When you do all the things that I commanded, you say, 'We are unprofitable servants. We have done only that which we ought to have done.' "

So you too. We are bought with a price by Jesus Christ. We are not our own. We are like the servant who was bought in the market. Paul said, "For not one of us lives for himself. And not one dies for himself. For if we live, we live for the Lord. Or if we die, we die for the Lord. Therefore, whether we live or die, we are the Lord's. For to this end, Christ died and lived again, that He might be Lord both of the dead and of the living." Many times we've thought that Jesus died for our sins. That's part of the truth. But also He died to be Lord of those for whom He died. Paul said again and again that we are not our own. We are the temple of the living God. Then, if we are bought, we are slaves, servants of Jesus Christ. Paul and Peter and James and the other New Testament authors were of this opinion. They thought it fitting to describe themselves as servants of Jesus Christ.

We were lost before we were found by the Lord. Lost in sin. We were going to eternal damnation. But there is

another truth: we are still lost. We have a change of
owner, but still we are lost. We were lost first in sin and in
the hands of Satan. Now we are lost in the hands of Jesus.
Many people think that when they were saved, they were
made free. They say, "Oh, praise the Lord, now I am free."
You are free from sin, but only to become slaves of
righteousness. Usually we think that we are free, and we
forget the other half of the truth. We were made free from
sin to be servants, or slaves, of righteousness.

### The Kingdom of God Versus the Kingdom of Darkness

Jesus came to the world to introduce the Kingdom.
We were born into the kingdom of darkness, the kingdom
of selfishness, the kingdom where everybody does his own
will. Satan has put a law on this kingdom. Paul told the
Ephesians that when we were unsaved we lived according
to the desires of our flesh and according to the dictation of
our thoughts. Satan, the prince of this world of darkness,
has made this law: you may live as you want in this world,
do what you please; there's plenty of freedom to do what
you like. But the world and the kingdom of darkness is like
a sinking ship that is going to end in the deepest ocean.

When the captain knows that the ship is lost, he goes
to the passengers and says to them, "Those of you who are
in second class may pass to first class without paying
anything. You are free to do that. Those of you who want
to drink may have all the whiskey you want. It's all free. If
you want to play soccer in the dining room, go ahead. If
you break the lamps, don't worry." The people say, "What
a nice captain we have. We can do whatever we want on
the ship." Nevertheless, they are all going to be sunk in the

deepest sea in a few minutes. It is the same in the kingdom of darkness. You can do whatever you want. You can have as much freedom as you want—drugs, sex, anything you think you desire. You think you are the king of your little kingdom, of your life, but you are led by the spirit of the world, and the spirit of this world is selfishness. You are lost.

Paul said that salvation means to be translated from one kingdom to the other. We have been translated from darkness into the kingdom of God. You are either in the kingdom of darkness or in the kingdom of light. But either way, you are not free. We call it freedom because we are free from darkness, but we are now under the rulership of Jesus Christ. In the kingdom of God, you cannot do your own will. This is the reason it is called the *kingdom* of God. He rules. He is the king, the governor. The Lord's Prayer says, "Thy kingdom come, Thy will be done. . . ." In this kingdom everybody does the will of the Lord. We cannot live according to our thoughts, but according to His thoughts. This is the main difference between these two kingdoms. Some people think the difference is we don't smoke, we don't drink, we don't go to the movies, or do other such things. But the real difference between these two kingdoms is that in the kingdom of darkness everybody does his own will, while in the kingdom of God everybody does God's will. The testimony of those who are really committed to the Lord, who have really passed from death to life, is this: Before I met Jesus I was ruling my own life, but since I've met Him, He rules.

Some people think and live as if there were three ways: *the wide way* for those who go to hell; *the narrow way* for those who are preachers and missionaries; and then a third way—not so wide but not so narrow—*the medium way* for the rest of the believers. Of course that is not in the book of doctrine, but it is the way people live. That medium way is an invention of man. Either we are in the kingdom of darkness doing our own will or we are in the kingdom of God doing His will.

A problem arises when we try to get free of the kingdom of darkness and get into God's kingdom. We are slaves of sin, and the only way to get free of slavery is death. When the slaves of the Old South sang, they usually sang about heaven. They sang, "I'll see Peter, I'll see John, I'll walk down the streets of gold and say hello to St. Paul." They sang about heaven because on this earth they had no freedom, no liberty at all. Their freedom came with death. As slaves of sin our only escape lies likewise in death . . . death to sin. But we run into a different problem in securing admission to the kingdom of God. A new birth is necessary. I am an Argentine. If I want to become an American all I have to do is fill out an application and fulfill some other requirements. But suppose that the laws of America said that in order to be an American you must be born on American soil. I would say, "Officer, I want to be an American."

"Where were you born?"

"In Buenos Aires, Argentina."

"Then you cannot be an American because you were not born in the United States of America."

"But how can I do it? I want so much to be an American."

"The only thing you can do is die, be born again—and be sure to be born an American. That's the only way.

We don't receive visitors. We don't accept visas any more."

That's the way it is with the kingdom of God. So how can a man change his citizenship? Jesus brought the solution. His death on the cross and His resurrection mean that any person who is a slave here, who looks to the cross of Jesus with faith, enters into the death of Jesus and so dies himself. Some people only think of the cross as a place where He died, but it is also the site of our own deaths. But it's not only death—it's also resurrection. It's the whole atonement of Jesus that we must understand and experience. We must look to Jesus not only to die, but also to be born again—into the new kingdom.

That is what water baptism really means. For a long time I was baptizing people as a ceremony. We brought photographers, we wore nice clothes, and the choir was singing in the background. It was all very nice. Now I understand that baptism should be done the very moment a person believes, not as a ceremonial recognition of conversion to be celebrated at a convenient moment. Baptism has meaning in itself. Some people baptize by immersion, others by sprinkling. I don't worry too much about the mode because in the Bible it is not plain. (The way to love one another is very plain, yet we don't do that—choosing rather to argue about the way we baptize.) But baptism by immersion shows His death and resurrection very plainly. We don't put the person into the water and leave him there. We raise him up again. When we baptize we do it in the name of the Lord. So it is as if God Himself is the One who is administering the baptism. Sometimes in Argentina we baptize people with this

formula: "I kill you in the name of the Lord. And I declare
you born into the kingdom of God to serve God and to
please Him." It's a different formula, and it works much
better. Some people think that baptism alone saves and
other people think that faith alone saves. But in truth no
baptism is authentic without faith, and faith finds fulfill-
ment in baptism.

Baptism is like a dollar bill. Every currency has two
types of value. One is its intrinsic value, the value of the
paper and the ink. On that basis a dollar bill is worth very
little. But though it is just paper and ink, it has a value.
Not because of the paper or the amount of ink, but
because it is an official certificate of the federal reserves of
the United States government.

So it is with baptism. The water and the ceremony by
themselves are of little consequence. But when they are
backed by Jesus' death and resurrection, they possess
great value to the person who knows that he is passing
from death to life.

In Argentina we try to baptize people at the time of
their conversion. If a person says, "I believe," but, when
we speak to him about baptism he then says, "Well, I will
wait," we doubt his commitment to God. One must obey
the Gospel to be saved and baptism is a clear test for
obedience. When we speak to a person about the Lord, we
explain about the two kingdoms, but we don't assure him
he is in this other kingdom until after he has come out of
the water. If we are not close to a river or pool, any
bathroom tub will do. We like to use a person's own
house, baptizing also his wife and children. They have
towels and heat, and then you can enjoy a cup of coffee

after the baptism. It's much more comfortable than in the church building.

When the new believer comes out of the water we say, "Brother, God is going to be your spiritual Father. You must obey Him because He is going to communicate to you all the commandments of Jesus Christ." It's a new life. When he comes up out of the water, he enters into another kingdom—the kingdom of God. The primitive church didn't just baptize the same day; they did it the same moment the people were converted. They didn't even wait for the meeting that night. If they were saved in the morning, baptism was done in the morning. If they were saved at midnight, as was the Philippian jailer, they were baptized at once. Baptism was held at the moment when the person really understood that he was escaping from darkness and being born into the kingdom of God.

The kingdom of God came to break into the kingdom of darkness. It must grow and grow until the kingdom of the world becomes the kingdom of our Lord and Savior, Jesus Christ.

## The Price of Citizenship

To enter the kingdom of God, we must die to ourselves. Many people want to keep on doing their own will even after they are saved. This is the reason Jesus says that those who want to save their own lives are going to lose them. And those who lose their lives are going to have them. Many people come to church wanting to live their own lives, but to live your own life means you are bypassing the will of Jesus.

The Bible says the kingdom of God is like a merchant looking for fine pearls. When he finds a pearl of real worth, he sells everything he has and buys that pearl. Of course, according to traditional thinking, man is the pearl of great price and Jesus the merchant who sells everything to make the purchase. Now I understand that *He* is the pearl of great price, and man the merchant.

So when man finds Jesus, it costs him everything. Jesus has happiness, joy, peace, healing, security, eternity. Man marvels at such a pearl and says, "I want this pearl. How much does it cost?"

The seller says, "It's too dear, too costly."

"But how much?"

"Well, it's very expensive."

"Do you think I could buy it?"

"Oh, of course. Anybody can."

"But you say it's too expensive. How much is it?"

"It costs everything you have—no more, no less—so anybody can buy it."

"I'll buy it."

"What do you have? Let's write it down."

"I have $10,000 in the bank."

"Good, $10,000. What else?"

"I have nothing more. That's all I have."

"Have you nothing more?"

"Well, I have some dollars here in my pocket."

"How many?"

"I'll see: 30, 40, 50, 80, 100, 120—120 dollars."

"That's fine. What else do you have?"

"I have nothing else. That's all."

"Where do you live?"

"I live in my house."

"The house too."

"Then you mean I must live in the garage?"

"Have you a garage, too? That too. What else?"

"Do you mean that I must live in my car, then?"

"Have you a car?"

"I have two."

"Both become mine. Both cars. What else?"

"Well, you have the house, the garage, the cars, the money, everything."

"What else?"

"I have nothing else."

"Are you alone in the world?"

"No, I have a wife, two children. . . ."

"Your wife and your children too."

"Too?"

"Yes, everything you have. What else?"

"I have nothing else, I am left alone now."

"Oh, you too. Everything. Everything becomes mine: wife, children, house, garage, cars, money, clothing, everything. And you too. Now you can use all those things here but don't forget they are mine, as you are. When I need any of the things you are using you must give them to me because now I am the owner."

When we started to preach and teach discipleship in our congregations we were so full of the spirit of truth that people were willing to obey. Many people, even me. I had a small apartment with only one bedroom, one dining room, bathroom, and kitchen. That's all. That represented our savings. In our country you cannot save money in the bank because inflation is too high. Sometimes it is eighty percent in one year, so you cannot possibly save money. Thus to save you have to buy something. So our apartment was our savings from all our life. But as soon as we understood the rulership of Jesus Christ, we put our apartment up for sale, thinking we would bring the money to the church. Other people in the congregation brought their homes—everything. We didn't know what to do with all these things. So the pastors met together.

"What shall we do?"

One said, "Perhaps we can sell all these houses and build a big, big building to have a big church in Buenos Aires."

Others said, "Oh, no, brother. We don't think that's the will of the Lord."

"But what shall we do with all these homes?"

After six months of prayer, God told us what to do. We called the people who had given pieces of real estate and the other things. We told them to come and take the things back. The Lord showed us that He didn't want our houses empty—He wanted houses with us inside. He wanted houses with carpets, heating, air-conditioning, and somebody who paid the light bills, telephone bills, put food on the tables and made the beds—for God. And He wanted our cars, with drivers. It meant that everything became His, even ourselves. So now all the houses are open. When visitors come to our congregation, we don't say, "Which one of you can take this brother to your house?" Because all houses are given to the Lord. We tell them, "Brother, come, you're going to take these people to your house." We command, we don't ask. Because the house is already given to the Lord. We just thank the Lord that He lets us live in His house.

We learned to have a different perspective. It's not

lending a house to God, it's God letting us use His house. When He needs the bed we must leave the bed and sleep on the floor. And God may use the bed for anyone He chooses because it's His. He's first, then me in that bed, or that kitchen, or wherever. In the kingdom of God, when a merchant finds a pearl of great price, he sells *everything* and buys it.

The kingdom is also like marriage. When a girl marries a boy, she becomes his. Likewise, all the things he has are hers. If he has two cars, both cars are hers too. If he has two houses, both become hers. However, even though she enjoys everything he has, she loses her name.

So it is in our encounter with Jesus. We become His, and everything He has becomes ours, only, sadly, we often forget to tell people that everything they have becomes His. There's no lordship if we don't surrender all.

Jesus said, "I would like you to be cold or hot. But because you are lukewarm I am going to spit you out of my mouth." What things do we vomit? We vomit the things that don't digest. If a thing is digested we won't vomit it. Vomited people are those people who don't want to be digested by the Lord Jesus Christ. Digestion means you get lost. You're finished. You end your life. You are transformed into Jesus.

One night I had a big steak in Dallas, Texas. It was very nice, almost as nice as those we have in Argentina. After I chewed the steak, it went into my stomach. There the gastric juice came quickly to dissolve the steak. The gastric juice said to the steak, "Good evening, how are you?"

"Fine, fine. What are you coming for?"

"I've come to dissolve you, to transform you into Juan Carlos Ortiz."

"Ah, no. Wait a minute. It's enough that he ate me. But to disappear completely—no, no, no! I don't mind being in his stomach, but I want to stay as steak. I don't want to lose my individuality, my personality. I want to maintain my steak identity."

"Sorry, sir. You must be dissolved and become Juan Carlos."

So there is a fight. Suppose the steak wins the fight and gastric juice lets him alone to be as a steak in my stomach. You know what will happen. Very soon that steak will be spewed out. That is the reason food is vomited—because it doesn't want to be dissolved.

But, suppose the steak lets the gastric juice dissolve him. The steak loses his identity but he gains Juan Carlos Ortiz's identity. Before I ate that steak, it was part of an unknown cow behind the hills. Nobody paid much attention to that cow. But because he let himself get dissolved, that steak is now writing a book and preaching on television.

So it is with us. We are in the Lord. In order to be in Jesus we must lose everything and become Jesus. That is the meaning of salvation: he who loses his life will have it. We must be Jesus in this world.

## The Lordship of Jesus

In Jesus' parable of the servant, He tells us that all our time is His. The eight hours we work, the eight hours we sleep, and the other eight hours also are His. Perhaps after we return home from our job we say, "Tonight I'll take a shower, look at television for a bit, and then go to bed. The pastor told me there would be a meeting tonight, but I deserve a rest. It's enough that I attend a church meeting once a week. I deserve. . . ."

You deserve what, Mr. Slave? We deserve nothing because we are servants. We were bought by Jesus Christ. All our hours belong to Him. The servant in Jesus' parable, while he was out in the field, was not thinking, "I'll take a shower when I get home, and then have a nice snack." No, he was thinking, "What shall I prepare for my master?" While he was plowing he thought, "Shall I fix him rice and beans? No, he had that yesterday. A steak with french fried potatoes? No, he doesn't like fried potatoes too much. Better baked potatoes." He was thinking of the master, not of himself.

We are more like the man who comes in from work and asks his wife, "Who's going to preach at church tonight?"

"Juan Carlos, I think."

"Ahh, then I needn't go."

But even if he did go the choir would have to sing nice . . . and the meeting not be too long. We see ourselves as the lords who sit in the pews and Jesus as our servant. We are all upside down. We say "Lord" with our mouth but by our attitude we call Him slave. "Lord, I'm going out in the car. Please drive the car. Don't let us crash."

"Yes, madam."

"Lord, my husband needs a better job because he's not earning enough."

"Yes, madam."

"Oh, help my child, he has examinations today. Please help, Lord. . . ."

Lord? Or servant? We should say "Lord" only when we are ready to give ourselves to Him and be His slaves. "Come on," He says, "prepare something for me to eat and properly clothe yourself and serve me until I have eaten and drunk and *afterward* you will eat and drink."

When we come home from a meeting my wife is wearing gloves, her high heels, and carrying a purse. But as soon as we get home, she lays down the gloves and purse, she takes off the high heels, puts on an apron, and serves me dinner. We cannot serve Jesus if we don't give ourselves as His servants. The satisfaction of the servant is to see the Lord satisfied. Everybody should be thinking what we shall bring Him for supper. Praises are part of the supper. Hymns are the water of the table. However, the offering is not always for the Lord. We sometimes say, "Let's raise an offering for the Lord so we can put air conditioning in the room." He doesn't need air conditioning—it's for us. Jesus said the only things that are given to Him are those things given to the poor. But even our gifts to the poor are only an appetizer for the Lord. The main dish Jesus eats is the lives of men.

We are to yield our bodies as a living sacrifice to Him. Then, when we have brought our own bodies to Him, we must bring the lives of others to Him as well. That's the main dish, the meat of the dinner. When the Lord sees us bringing somebody else to Him, He says, "My servant is coming with food." Even the angels in heaven sing when we bring others under the lordship of Jesus Christ. If we don't gird ourselves, Jesus cannot be served.

Jesus ends His story by saying, "Does the master thank the slave because he did the things which were commanded of him?" No, says Jesus. We don't need to be thanked for the things we do. "So you too, when you do all the things which are commanded, can only say, 'We are unworthy slaves. We have done only that which we ought to have done.' " Can anyone say, "I have done everything that God commanded?" If that is so, we are ready for a graduation ceremony. When a person does everything the Lord commands, He gives him a diploma. And the diploma reads: *unprofitable servant.*

But we are so upside down today that *we* call ourselves the "reverends." Once I heard the announcer in a meeting introduce the preacher saying, "And now, the great servant of God." The organ played and the spotlights focused as the "great servant" appeared. But if he is great, he is not a servant. And if he is a servant, he is not great. "Come, gird thyself and serve me until I have eaten and drunk and after that ye shall eat and drink." Our eating will be in heaven. And here on earth our eating and our refreshment and our joy will be when we see Jesus satisfied with our work for Him. He is the Lord, and we are His servants.

# CHAPTER 6

# He Is King

**The Names of Jesus**

Jesus has many names. The Word of God labels Him: Jesus, Savior, Christ, the Messiah, the Anointed, the Authorized One (to do the things He did), the Love of God, the Lion of Judah, the Star of the Morning, the Son of Righteousness, the Cloud of Glory, the Water of Life. He's everything. Jesus is so inclusive that no one name can tell everything about Him.

He is lamb and lion at the same time. He is fire and water at the same time. He is cloud and He is rock. He is everything in the universe. But even though He has many names, Paul says that He has one name that is above all other names. And at the announcement of that name every knee shall bow, and every tongue confess that Jesus Christ is Lord.

What does the word *Lord* mean? In my language, Spanish, we say "lord" to everybody. We don't have two words to match lord and mister—there is only one, señor. When we say Señor Smith, Señor Williams, and Señor Jesus, it is the same as saying Lord Smith, Lord Williams —or Mister Smith, Mister Williams, and Mister Jesus. The word has lost its meaning in Spanish because there is no distinction.

However, when I came among the English speaking

people I found the same problem even though English has two words. Perhaps it is because of the condition of the lords of England's nobility. Whatever the reason, the word lord doesn't mean what it once meant. The word *Lord* used to bespeak authority—it referred to the one who was above all others. Today the word bears very little sense of authority.

In the days of Jesus, the word "lord" (*kurios*—with lower case letters) was what slaves called their masters. When it appeared in capital letters—THE LORD—it meant the Caesar of Rome. As a matter of fact, when public employees or soldiers met each other they used to greet one another by calling out "Caesar is the Lord," and the other responding "Yes, the Lord is Caesar."

This presented a problem for the Christians. They insisted to the contrary that Jesus Christ is the Lord. Caesar did not mind other men being called lords as long as the term "THE LORD" was reserved for him. But the Christians reserved the term for Jesus. They placed Jesus high above the emperor. They said, in effect, "Caesar, you can count on us in some things, but when Jesus and you are in the balance, we will stay with Jesus, because we have committed our lives to Him. He is the first one. He is THE LORD—the one who possesses supreme authority over us." That was the reason Caesar persecuted the Christians.

## A Man-Centered Gospel

The gospel that we have in the Bible is the gospel of the kingdom of God. The gospel that presents Jesus as King, as Lord, as First One, as the Maximum Authority.

The gospel of the kingdom is the Christ-centered gospel. But there is another gospel—the gospel we have been hearing these last centuries. It's the gospel centered in man and not in Christ, in the human and not in the divine. This gospel is a consequence of a humanistic tide that came on this world. The church let humanism come into her and now we have received this humanistic gospel—this gospel centered in man. I call it "the gospel of the offers," "the gospel of the big sales," "the gospel of the specials," where the preacher offers the people some incentive to accept Jesus. But we don't accept Jesus, it is Jesus who accepts us. The preacher presents Jesus as the one who is knocking at the door, and he says to the people, "Please open the door to Him." So the man thinks that he is going to do Jesus a great favor if he opens the door for Him. That is the gospel of the offers. If you accept Jesus, the preacher says, you are going to have joy, peace, health, and prosperity.

Such a gospel appeals to the interest of man, not the interest of Jesus. "If you bring $10, you are going to get $20," we are told. Jesus is presented as *my* personal Savior and Healer, and as the King who is coming for *me*. Because *me* is the center of this gospel we have been preaching.

Our meetings are man-centered. Even the way the furniture is placed in the meeting room—the chairs, the pulpit, the Bible—is focused on man's needs and not on God. When the pastor makes the program for the meeting, he thinks first about the needs of the people rather than the desire of God. "Now the first hymn will be standing, the second will be seated, because the people are going to be tired. Then we can have a duet just to change the atmosphere a little bit. And now we are going to have . . .

and now . . . and now . . . and all this must be within one hour because people will get tired." The whole program is made thinking of the people, not of Jesus Christ the Lord.

We sing hymns for us and about *us*. "Give me, help me, bless me."

Our prayers are also humanistic, man-centered: "Lord, give me, help me, bless my home, bless my husband, bless my cat, bless my dog . . . mine, me, Amen. Oh yes, for Jesus' sake." But that's not for Jesus' sake, that's for our sake. Prayer becomes a kind of Aladdin's lamp. Use it and you will receive everything you like. No wonder Karl Marx said religion is the opiate of the people. Perhaps he was right, for it's quite possible for this gospel to become an escape, an opiate. Jesus Christ, though, is not an opiate. He is the Lord! And it takes a real man to come and give himself to Jesus when He speaks as Lord.

Our prayers, as we have seen, are man-centered. The prayers in the Bible, however, are God-centered; see Nehemiah, Daniel, or Acts. Look at that prayer the primitive church prayed when they were threatened by the police and by the high priest because they were preaching Jesus Christ. Afterward they went to their people and told how they were threatened with whippings and death if they preached about Jesus. "And when they heard that, they lifted up their voices to God with one accord, and said, Lord, thou art God, which has made heaven, and earth, and the sea, and all that in them is: who by the mouth of thy servant David hast said, Why did the heathen rage, and the people imagine vain things? The kings of the earth stood up, and the rulers were gathered together against the Lord, and against his Christ. For of a truth against thy holy child Jesus, whom thou

hast anointed, both Herod, and Pontius Pilate, with the
Gentiles, and the people of Israel, were gathered together,
for to do whatsoever thy hand and thy counsel determined
before to be done. And now, Lord, behold their threaten-
ings: and grant unto thy servants, that with all boldness
they may speak thy word, by stretching forth thine hand to
heal; and that signs and wonders may be done by the
name of thy holy child Jesus. And when they had prayed,
the place was shaken where they were assembled together;
and they were all filled with the Holy Ghost . . ." (Acts 4:
24–31). It couldn't happen any other way.

If we were threatened by the police and the high
priest, our prayers would be something like this: "Oh,
Father, be merciful to us. Help us, Lord. Be merciful to
Peter and John. Don't let the people lay their hands upon
them. Please, give us a way of escape. Don't let us suffer.
Look what they are doing to us. Oh, Lord, meet them and
don't let them do us any harm." Us, me, we, I. A
man-centered gospel.

All this is not just a matter of semantics, it is a matter
of attitude. It is the basic problem in the church. It is not
enough for us to change our vocabulary and use the word
*thou* instead of *me*. We must change our minds. God must
take out our brains and wash them in detergent and brush
them and turn them around and then put them back,
because we have a wrong attitude.

## A God-Centered Gospel

In ancient times people thought the earth was the
center of the universe and the sun was going around
the earth. They were, as we now know, wrong. But are we

really much different than our ancient ancestors? We think
we are the center of the universe, and God and Jesus
Christ and the angels are around us for our benefit.
Heaven is for us, we sing. The angels are for us. Jesus is for
us. God is for us. It's all there for us. We are wrong; God
is the center, and we are around Him. We sing "Jesus
belongs to me," "I am satisfied with Jesus." But God is
calling us to sing a new song. *He* is the center. He is the
Sun, and we are the earth that is going around the Sun.

In Bible School days our director sometimes brought
in a speaker to move our hearts for evangelism. He would
preach about the lost souls. He would say, "Oh, young
men, look at the lost souls. They are perishing. They're
going into hell. Each time the clock strikes one, 5,822½
persons go to hell. Are you not sorry for them?"

It was not for Jesus' sake, but for the lost souls' sake.
It sounded nice, but it was wrong. We are not going to
save souls because of the souls. We are going to extend the
kingdom of God because God says so and He is the Lord.
Our motivations must be cleaned up.

Many of us like to preach against smoking. If you
were supposed to smoke, we say, God would have made a
chimney in your head. We say, "You shouldn't smoke
because the smoke harms your lungs and cancer is brought
on by smoking." But once again our appeal is man-
centered. Listen, if Jesus said don't smoke—even if
smoking would cure cancer—we should quit smoking.

I call this gospel the fifth gospel. We have the gospels
of St. Matthew, St. Mark, St. Luke, and St. John, and now
a fifth, the gospel of St. Evangelicals. The gospel according
to St. Evangelicals is taken from verses here and there in
the other four gospels. We take one verse here, one verse

there, all the verses that offer something, all the verses of promise like John 3:16 and John 5:24, putting all these verses together to form a systematic theology on salvation. Then we forget the other verses, the demands of Jesus Christ. This is the fifth gospel, the gospel of the offers, the gospel that presents Jesus as a personal Savior—only.

Who authorized us to present Jesus as this or as that and not as He really is? Suppose a young couple is getting married. And when the pastor asks the groom, "Will you take this woman to be your wife?" the young man says, "Pastor, I accept this girl as my personal cook, dishwasher, and maid." What would the girl say? She would say, "Wait a moment. I'm going to cook, yes. And I'm going to wash dishes. I'm going to clean the house. But I'm not a maid. I'm going to be your wife, and you also have to give me your love, your heart, your home—everything." That's marriage!

It's the same with Jesus. It's true He is the Savior. Then we get spiritual and accept Him as healer too. Wait a moment. He is what He is. We cannot cut Jesus into pieces and take the piece we like best. We are like children who are given bread with jam. They eat the jam and give you back the bread. Then you put more jam on it and they lick off the jam again and give you back the bread. That's the way we want to do with Jesus. We want to take the jam and give the bread away. We have to eat the bread with the jam. Heaven may be the jam, but the Lord Jesus is the Bread of Life.

Most people come to church because they want to go to heaven and flee from hell. If all the preachers and teachers one day told their people, "We have decided that there is no heaven or hell," how many would stay in the church after that? Most of the people would ask, "Why are we coming then?" They were coming for heaven, not because Jesus is Lord and everybody must submit to Him. Others came because they wanted to get healed.

And what was the real message on that famous day of Pentecost when everyone spoke in tongues? God's message for that hour was not that everyone should speak in tongues. Rather it was "And he that you have crucified, God made him Lord and Christ." That was the message: God made Him *Lord* and *Christ*. When people heard this, they started to tremble.

"Is He the Lord now?"

"Yes."

"What shall we do then? We are lost!"

"Don't worry, repent and be baptized for the remission of your sins and you will receive the Holy Spirit."

*Lord.* The Bible says that if we call upon the name of the Lord Jesus Christ, that is, if we come under the lordship of Jesus Christ, we shall be saved. The Bible also says that with the heart a person believes. If you believe in your heart, and you confess with your mouth that Jesus Christ is the Lord, you shall be saved. He is much more than a Savior, He is the Lord.

An example of the fifth gospel can be found in the usual application of Luke 12:32. "Do not be afraid little flock, for your Father hath chosen gladly to give you the kingdom." Many of us love to preach from this verse. But what about the next verse? "Sell your possessions and give to charity." Never have I heard a sermon preached on this. Why? Because this verse is not in the fifth gospel. Yet this verse is a commandment. In it Jesus explains the meaning of verse 32. Sell your possessions and give alms.

Who has an option with reference to commandments? No one, they are compulsory. Yet the fifth gospel has made some things optional: you don't have to if you don't want to. But that is not the gospel of the kingdom, that is the gospel of the offers.

We read in the Bible, "Come unto me all ye that are weary and heavy laden and I will give you rest." That too is often preached. But, "Take my yoke upon you and learn of me (be humble)"—that is not frequently preached, for it is not in the fifth gospel. The fifth gospel says we lose our burdens and problems when we are saved. But the gospel of the kingdom says you get free of this yoke in order to get another yoke—the Jesus yoke. He needs you free of all burdens so He can use you for His kingdom. He wants to deliver you from your problems that you may have His problems. Why? Because we have to live for the King and not for ourselves.

Many of my friends have underlined verses in their Bibles, most of which compose the fifth gospel. To see what I mean, read the verses you have *never* underlined, because that is the truth you lack. I do not underline the Bible any more because the underline divides the verses into first class and second class. I used to have my Bible underlined with many colors. Now I have everything the same color, because every word is important.

### Jesus' Gospel

In the Old Testament, Jesus was always presented as the coming King, the coming Lord, greater than Moses, greater than David, greater than the angels. Even David

said, "The Lord said to my Lord, sit at my right hand."
Jesus was always presented as Lord. Humble as He was,
He never left a shadow of doubt that He was the Lord.
Look how He introduced Himself to Zaccheus. Zaccheus
was up in a tree and Jesus was down under it. As soon as
Jesus saw him, He said, "Zaccheus!" Now we twentieth-
century preachers, trying to win Zaccheus for Christ,
would have probably said, "Are you Mr. Zaccheus? It's
nice to meet you. I would like to say a few words to you,
sir. Would you look at your calendar and when it is
convenient for you, I would like to have an appointment."

That would leave Zaccheus a choice, and he would
say, "Well, is it very important?"

"Well, that depends. I think it's very important, but
perhaps you wouldn't agree."

"Well, let's see, mmmmm, oh, it's all filled up. Next
week, maybe." Jesus never said that. No, He said,
"Zaccheus, hurry. Come down, because I need to go to
your house today." Jesus never gave a choice to anybody
because salvation is not a choice—it is a commandment.

Zaccheus was commanded to come down from the
tree. He had to obey or disobey. Such commands immediately divide men into two camps. The one who is
disobedient becomes an enemy of Jesus. His friends show
themselves by their obedience.

So Zaccheus obeyed. He lost no time jumping down,
and Jesus and the apostles went to his house. As soon as
Zaccheus got to his home he said to his wife, "Honey,
please prepare some food for these people."

"Oh, darling, why didn't you tell me you had invited
people to come and eat?"

"Darling, I didn't invite them, they invited themselves." Jesus doesn't need an invitation. He's the Lord of all houses and all people.

Zaccheus knew that Jesus was Lord and the Lord had come for him. So he announced that he would give half his goods to the poor and restore fourfold all he had cheated people of. Then Jesus said, "Today salvation has come to this house." Jesus didn't explain to him God's plan of salvation. Jesus didn't explain to him the four spiritual laws. He didn't even show him the "Roman Road" to salvation. He just said, "Hurry, come down!" When did Zaccheus get saved? When he obeyed. Because obedience brings a person under the lordship of Jesus Christ. Not the acceptance of a philosophy, but the obedience to a commandment brings salvation.

The same thing happened with Matthew. He was collecting taxes. Jesus didn't stand beside him waiting until Matthew looked His way so He could say, "Hello, I'm Jesus. It's awfully nice to meet you. But keep on working, I know you are busy. I can wait." No. That would have given the choice to Matthew. Jesus said, "Matthew, follow me!" It was a commandment, not an invitation. Matthew had to obey or disobey. This is the gospel of the kingdom. The kingdom of God is at hand: repent, and believe the gospel. And the word *believe* means obey!

The same thing happened to the rich young ruler. "Good master, what must I do to be saved?"

After hearing of the young man's strict obedience to the ten commandments, Jesus said, "Well, one thing you lack. Sell all that you have and distribute to the poor, and you will have treasure in heaven; and come, follow me."

He went home sad. If we had been there, we would have run after the young ruler and said, "Listen, don't take it so seriously. Jesus didn't mean it that way. He'll soften up once He understands how much you have. Why not start with just a part of what you have. You can increase it next year and won't even miss it." We would have invited him to follow Jesus, but on his own terms, not Jesus' terms. That is why Jesus let him go. He loved him, but if He had lowered the requirements, that man never could have been saved—from himself.

To another Jesus said, "Follow me." But he said, "Lord, let me first go and bury my father." We would have said, "Of course, of course. Forgive me, I didn't know. Take two or three days." No! Jesus said, "Leave the dead to bury their own dead; but as for you, go and proclaim the kingdom of God." *I will follow* cannot be followed by a *but*. Who is first but Jesus? Here is another person who wanted to follow Jesus on his own terms, but Jesus said, "No, it's on my terms."

We are not saved because we agree to a certain formula or philosophy; we are saved because we do what God says. Jesus said to others, "Follow me!" They didn't say, "Follow you where? How much are you going to pay us?" They never asked because they knew Jesus would reject them.

God commands all men to repent. If people don't repent they are disobedient to God. For this reason there is a punishment and a chastisement for people who don't repent. God wouldn't punish us if He had just invited us to come. But He commanded us. That is why there is a punishment.

Suppose you say to me, "Brother, would you like to have a piece of cake?"

"Oh, no, thank you," I reply.

Then pow! Pow!

"Why are you whipping me?"

"You didn't take the cake."

"But you just invited me to take the cake, you didn't command me. If you had commanded me then you would have a reason for being angry, but you only invited me."

Salvation is not an invitation; it is a command. We cannot please God if we do not believe it, and we cannot believe it without obeying it.


## Jesus Is Lord

Jesus taught us to pray "Thy kingdom come, Thy will be done on earth as it is in heaven." What does this mean? I am the king of my life; I am seated on the throne; I make the decisions. But when Jesus comes I must abdicate my throne and let Him sit on the throne. The testimony of those who are really in the kingdom of God is all the same: "Till I met Jesus, I was the commander of my life. Since I met Him, He commands."

"Thy will be done on earth" is something for here and now—not for tomorrow, not the ages to come. Not only do we have a fifth gospel, but we have offered it in comfortable monthly payments. The used-car salesman says, "You can have the car for fifty dollars." It sounds good, but he really means fifty dollars down with monthly payments thereafter. We do the same thing with the gospel. We tell people, "All you have to do to be saved is raise your hand." We don't tell them that is just the first payment. After a while we say to them, "Now we are going to have a nice warm day when spring comes and we are going to heat the water, and perhaps you would like to take advantage of this and be baptized." That was not the message of the primitive church. The early church was more forthright than we are.

Then after a while we ask for the third payment. "You know that in order to support all the things here, we pay tithes. But if that is asking too much, perhaps you'd prefer to start with 5% and move up to the tithe next year. But if you tithe, God is going to give you threefold. In fact, the person who tithes has more than the one who doesn't." Sorry, that's a man-centered gospel.

Sadly, today's church members have been vaccinated against the true gospel with these small watered-down doses we give them once in a while. That is the reason we have people to whom we preach and preach and preach but who never respond. They are immune—vaccinated.

Jesus said, "Seek ye first the kingdom of God and His righteousness and all these things shall be added unto you." What were the things that Jesus promised were going to be added? The text is plain. We are going to receive the elementary things of life: food, drink, clothes, a house, the things we need. If we don't have these things, it is because we are not seeking first the kingdom of God. I learned long ago I don't have to worry about getting "these things." I worry about seeking the kingdom. Where do I get all these things? Well, they are added unto me while I am seeking the kingdom. As a result I have all I need.

If a person from another planet were to come to earth and see how Christians live, he would conclude that Jesus

had said something like this: "Seek ye first what you are
going to eat. Seek ye first how you are going to dress.
Which house are you going to buy? Which car are you
going to drive? Which girl are you going to marry? Which
job are you going to do? And then if there is a little time
left, and if it is not too uncomfortable for you, please do
something for the kingdom of God." That's the way most
of the people in the church live.

Once I asked a man, "What are you working for?"

He said, "If I do not work I do not eat."

"Well, what do you eat for?"

"Well, I eat to work to be able to eat to be able to
work that I may eat that I may be able to work to eat to
work."

That's not life, even though most people live like that.
These people are alive only because they are not dead.
They just breathe.

One day I finally understood the purpose of my life.
Now I know why I eat. I know why I work. I know why I
sleep. *I have a purpose.* That purpose is to extend the
kingdom. Our purpose is that God may govern over all the
human race. Jesus said, "All authority is given unto me in
heaven and in earth. Go therefore and make disciples. . . ."

That is the commandment of Jesus Christ. That is
what I live for, the kingdom, to conquer one home for
God, then another, and another. Inch by inch I must
recover the things that belong to God. And to do that I
have to eat, and to eat I have to work. But I work to be
able to eat to be able to work for the kingdom of God.
That is my purpose in life.

God's people do not go to the university because they

want to get a diploma and have a profession. They go to the university first of all because God put them there as members of His body to do His kingdom business in the university. As a bonus, they receive a diploma. God's people work for Ford Motor Company because God needs them in that spot of this earth as His soldiers to conquer that place for Him. And Mr. Ford gives them the money to do that job. And if we seek first the kingdom of God and His righteousness, then all these things shall be added unto us.

# CHAPTER 7

# Steps in Discipleship

## Members of the Church

> For just as we have many members in one body and all the members do not have the same function, so we, who are many, are one body in Christ, and individually members one of another (Romans 12:4 NASB).

> From whom (speaking of Christ) the whole body, being fitted and held together by that which every joint supplies, according to the proper working of each individual part, causes the growth of the body for the building up of itself in love (Ephesians 4:16 NASB).

What we call a member of the church today is quite different from the type of membership we read of in the Bible. I have studied many books about local church membership, and have found that almost all churches have three common requirements: 1) Attend the meetings; 2) Pay tithes and offerings to the church; 3) Live an upright life. Therefore, we say, if a person attends the meetings, pays tithes and offerings, and lives a life of holiness, he is a good member of the church. However, if we gave that definition to Paul I'm afraid he would say, "That is not a body-type member; that is a club-type member. For club members attend the club, pay the monthly dues, and abide by the rules. Body-type membership is another thing."

When I discovered I was pastor of a club rather than a New Testament church, I began a serious study of the Gospels and the Acts of the Apostles to see if I could find justification for what I called membership. There was none. I didn't even find the word "member." But reading the Acts I found another word thar really revolutionized my life and the life of our church. The word was *disciples*. This led us on a quest. We learned that a disciple is one who learns to live the life his teacher lives. Then, with his life, he teaches others to live the life he lives.

## Discipleship: a Communication of Life

Discipleship is not a communication of knowledge, but a communication of life. Jesus said, "The word I have spoken unto you, the language I speak to you, is not a letter word in language: it is life; it is spirit." In a discipleship relationship I do not teach the other person to know what I know, rather I teach him to become what I am. Discipleship, then, is not a communication of knowledge, but a communication of life and spirit. Making a disciple is different from winning a soul. Paul made disciples by living a life that taught others how to live. He said, "You must be like me, be imitators of me." For this reason, in order to start discipleship in the church, we ourselves must first be disciples. We must, for example, have good family and home relations, good parent-child relations, and good relations with our neighbors.

We all know the way things commonly work in the church. A pastor can have a fight with his wife and then go to the pulpit and speak about home relationships. But he cannot do that when he is making disciples. The disciples get into your home, they see how you live, and they seek to live the way you live. You teach more by living than by talking.

If I were to have a guest living or traveling with me for a week and he were to say to me, "Listen, Juan Carlos, I have been with you for a week and you have not taught me anything. Please, sit down and teach me," I would say, "Listen, if you have not learned anything from me by now I have nothing to teach you." Discipleship is not by talking but by living.

A study of the life of Jesus indicates there are three ways to teach: information, formation, and revelation.

## Information

All of us are familiar with informational teaching. We've used it for years in church and Sunday school. It is nothing more than passing along information. How many books in the Bible? Sixty-six. Which is the Psalm of the Good Shepherd? The 23rd. Who is Moses? Who is Abraham? We know their stories because we were informed. We know there is a church, a heaven, and a hell. There are angels, seraphs, and cherubs. We know the story of Paul. We know how Satan fell. We know all this because we were informed. Most Bible studies are information-type teaching. Now information is not bad, but it's the minimum way of teaching. Its basic ministry is simply to inform and in so doing to awake an interest in the things you are informed about.

Unfortunately, the church had made informational

teaching an end in itself. We know the words of the Bible, the books of the Bible, the history of the Bible, the teachings of the Bible. But we know them for no higher purpose than showing off our knowledge to one another. Information is good as a means, but not as an end.

Jesus almost never used this method of teaching. Can you imagine Jesus saying to his disciples, "Now don't forget tomorrow morning from 8:00 to 9:00 we have devotions. From 9:00 to 10:00 we will study the Minor Prophets. And from 10:00 to 11:00 we are going to have poetry, and then from 11:00 to 12:00 we will study rhetoric, homiletics, and hermeneutics?" Yet Jesus prepared the best ministers that history has known.

Many of our Bible studies, instead of making things simple and clear, make them more confused. In Bible School I was Professor of Romans. I was told Romans was such an important book it should be taught verse by verse. That is what I did, and it took me a whole year to teach Romans. I taught Romans in such a way that after a year of my lectures none of my students could remember what Romans was all about. I shudder when I recall my method.

Suppose I am in Rome and write a letter to my friend Bob Mumford. It opens, "Dear Brother Bob, I write this letter to you from Rome. I have arrived with my wife and children and we have seen this and that. . . ." And I write a long letter.

When Bob receives the letter he quickly goes to church and he says, "Brethren, we have received a letter from Brother Juan Carlos Ortiz. I have talked to the Committee on Religious Education and they agree we should study this letter at length. Therefore, during the next three months we will study the Epistle of Juan Carlos."

So the first Sunday all the people gather and Bob begins his teaching. "The letter starts like this, 'Dear Brother Bob.' 'Dear' in the Greek means a person who is loved. So when Bob is very dear, he means *loved one. Dear, dear.* I can imagine my brother Juan taking the pen and saying *dear.* His heart is overflowing with love. His wife is beside him joining him in love. How do you write your letters? Do you put *dear* in your letters? Come on, all of us must start saying *dear!* Let us say it in unison. Dear. Dear. Dear. But wait, there is more. 'Dear Bob.' Bob, he calls me by my name. He knows me. He really means it when he writes it because he says *Dear Bob.* Do you say *dear,* and do you call people by name? 'I write.' He himself is writing! He doesn't have a secretary. He has nobody who writes for him. Well, next Thursday we are going to continue with the Epistle of Juan Carlos. Now let's stand for our closing prayer."

So next Thursday comes. " 'I write from Rome.' Rome! The city founded by Romulus and Remus, whom the wolves fed. It was the capital city of the Roman Empire, built on seven hills. The Roman Empire was divided in two, the eastern and the western divisions. Many scholars believe that Rome did not fall because of its lack of military strength, but because of moral decay. Now, next verse." And the people say, "Ah, our pastor really goes deep. With one verse he can have two or three classes. What a tremendous pastor. What a scholar!"

Yet after three or four months spent picking apart the Epistle of Juan Carlos, nobody knows what that letter

really said. That's the way we teach the Bible. I imagine
that when we get to heaven, Paul will call most of us Bible
teachers over to one side and say, "Listen, I never said
what you taught."

Today, I no longer read just part of an epistle. I sit
down and read the whole letter. And I'm learning many
more lessons now than before.

Once I preached eight sermons, a whole series in a
whole week and twice on Sunday, from one single verse.
People said, "Oh, Brother Ortiz, where did you study? In
Germany? At Yale? Princeton?"

"No, no," I said humbly, "I went to the Bible School
here in Argentina."

"Oh, I thought you studied somewhere else. You are
so deep." But it was the deepness of nothing. I was only
disseminating information to impress others with my
learning.

## Formation

Jesus' favorite method of teaching His disciples was
through *formation*. Formation comes not by telling people
things they should know, but by commanding them to do
specific things. Jesus said to the disciples, "Go to such-
and-such city. Don't say hello, don't greet anybody in the
way. When you get to a house say, 'The peace of God be
on this house.' Heal the sick that are in the house. Eat
what they give you. Announce that the kingdom of God is
at hand, and don't pass from house to house. And if they
don't receive you in the house, go on to the next house."
Jesus didn't preach inspirational sermons; those are for
disobedient people, to convey to them that it would be

nice if they would like to do the thing Jesus commanded. So we preach the inspirational message, and while the organ plays and the choir sings, we try to coax people to make decisions—but a decision to what? Jesus didn't suggest or plead; He gave commands.

If we would be under the lordship of Jesus Christ, we must be *like* Him. This is the difference between preaching a personal Savior and preaching the Lord Jesus Christ. When we are under lordship it is, "Just say the word, Lord, and thy servant will do it." We don't need inspirational sermons.

Jesus didn't have to preach to His disciples, "Oh, disciples, the lost souls—each time the clock strikes, 5,952½ people go to hell! Don't you feel sorry for them? Don't you hear them shouting from hell?"

Jesus said, "Go to that city. Knock at the door. Say, 'The peace of God be over you.' Heal the people. *Go!*" He commanded. He didn't say, "Would you like to go?" He said, *Go!*

Formational teaching forms lives through specific command. It requires that we stop being speakers and start being fathers. A father is a man who has children, and a good father has obedient children. Learning doesn't come by hearing, but by obeying. Obedience is the key to learning in the kingdom of God.

If He is the Lord, I do what He commands. If we would be good fathers, we must command our children and see to it that they obey us. As it is the people hear our sermons and say, "Very nice. Thank you so much, pastor." Very nice, eh? That's all.

Jesus got a different reaction because He used a different method. When His disciples came back from their mission, He corrected them. They said, "Lord, even the demons were submissive to us."

He answered, "Don't rejoice in this alone; rejoice that your names are written in the Book of Life."

"Oh," they said. "We didn't know. Thank You."

"Jesus, there is a city that did not accept us. We decided that fire should come from heaven and kill them all."

"You don't know of which spirit you are. I didn't come to lose people but to save them."

"Forgive us, Lord."

Another time Peter came, "Jesus, speaking of Your death, that should never happen to You."

"Get away from me, Satan," Jesus shot back.

Tell that to one of the members of your congregation, and see what happens. Even rebuking is a part of the teaching process in discipleship.

## Formation by Submission

Here is the first law of discipleship: There will be no formation of life without submission. The club-type members don't submit. It's the other way. They want the pastor to submit to them. They have the annual general assembly of the club where they vote. In this way each year the pastor must be approved by the people. In the "new Bible" the pastor is submitted to the members, but my Bible says that the people should be submitted to the pastor.

Submission means submission, nothing less. I can form the life of my children because they submit to me. But if each time I corrected them I knew they could run away, it would be a different matter. If they could go to

another father saying, "I no longer want to be a child of
Juan Carlos Ortiz. I want to be a child of yours," and the
other father would say, "Oh, welcome, welcome," then my
correction would be constantly frustrated. But I'm sure
they are going to stay in my home, at least while they are
young and have nowhere else to go. That, by the way, is
the time to teach them. Correction is not rejection but an
expression of deeply caring love. The average pastor,
though, does not form lives because he is afraid to lose his
members. If he is too hard with a member, that member
may leave the church and look for another father (or
should I say join another orphanage?). We cannot form
life if we do not have submission.

Paul says to Titus, "This *speak, exhort,* and *rebuke*
with all authority." We first have to speak. If the speaking
is not obeyed, we exhort them. And if by exhorting
nothing happens, we'll rebuke them with all authority.
That is the way to form life and make disciples. People
don't know the harm they do themselves by not submitting. They become spoiled children.

Suppose we used the same system to form our
children's lives that we use in the church? Suppose I would
say to my children, "Children, it's time for the service. The
sermon today is going to be about washing the head.
Come on. Sit down, children. We're going to speak today
about soap and head. First we're going to sing a nice
chorus. The chorus is like this, 'Soap is a wonderful thing,
wonderful, wonderful. And when it's mixed with the
water, makes bubbles flow, flow, flow.' Do you like it? Isn't
it your favorite? Now the message: Soap is a product
invented in China four centuries before Christ. It comes in
bars of different sizes and colors and perfumes. When

soap, which is made of caustic elements and mineral, vegetable or animal oils is mixed with water and applied to the head, it cleanses. Of course, if it falls in the eyes, it burns. If a person takes care it won't burn, but even if it burns, it doesn't do too much harm. And so one has a clean head. And now while the organ plays softly and the choir sings, 'Just As I Am,' if anyone of you has been touched, if you want to wash your head, please raise your hands." My children would never raise their hands.

This is not the way to form lives. Do you know how my mother did with me? She said, "Johnny, please come and wash your hands." I said, "No, mommy, I think they're clean." "Come on, Johnny, they're not clean. Wash your hands." "No, mommy, tomorrow." Then she took me by the elbow, pushed me to the sink, and she washed my hands. She was forming my life. Thanks to that, I now wash them by myself. That's formational teaching.

Suppose I were to preach a sermon to the children, "Come children, today the message is on school. School is an organization invented by the angels in the sixth century before Christ. Now if you want to go to school, while the organ plays, raise your hand." No, we just send them to school. And that's all. Because we are forming lives. That is the way Jesus taught the disciples—by formation.

**Formation by Authority**

The second law of discipleship is: One cannot submit to a person who is himself unsubmitted. You control your disciples—but who controls you? You rebuke your disciples—but who rebukes you?

A Roman soldier, a centurion, came to Jesus because

one of his men was sick. Jesus told him, "I'm going to your home and I'm going to heal him."

The centurion said, "Jesus, I am not worthy. Do not come to my home. Just say the word and my boy shall recover. I understand this because I am also a man under authority. I tell a man go, and he goes; come, and he comes; do this, and he does it. So say the word and my son shall be healed." What did he mean by this? He meant that in order to have authority, you must be under authority. The source of all authority is God (Romans 13).

I cannot create authority in my own life. To have authority I must be in line with God and those whom God puts over me—maybe one, two, or three between God and me. But if I am in line, authority will pass through me to others. If I am not in line, I won't have authority.

A sergeant tells his soldiers, "Come here," and they come. "Go," he commands, and they go. So suppose the sergeant gets excited. "How about that. Look how much power I have! I will resign from the army and form an army of my own in my neighborhood." So he resigns and goes to his neighborhood, "I say, boys, come here."

"You come here, if you want us."

"Come on, do this."

"Do it yourself."

What happened? He lost his authority because he was no longer under authority. We want to have authority, but we want to be independent at the same time. That's impossible. You can't be independent and have authority. To have authority you must be under somebody else. Paul said to Timothy, "What you have seen and heard from me, teach to faithful men that they may teach others" (2 Tim.

2:2). It is a chain, one submitted to the other, and teaching another who is in turn submitted to him.

Being a disciple and being a member of the church according to the club-type of membership are very different things. When we understood this in Argentina, we said to the people, "We are no longer going to use the word 'member.' We are going to use instead the word 'disciple.' However, a disciple is one who obeys commands, so we all have a long way to go." We buried the word "member." And we started to use the word "disciple," even though we knew that none of us were yet disciples. But at least we were on the way.

## Making Disciples

How did we do it? I preached discipleship for months, before I started practicing it. Then one day, reading the Gospel according to Matthew, I saw that Jesus said all the multitudes were like sheep without a shepherd, and He chose twelve disciples. I said to myself, "It's time for a change." I had a club-type congregation. It was like an orphanage and I was The Reverend Juan Carlos Ortiz, director of the orphanage. When I realized this, I decided to start a new underground church in my home. And Johnny stole a group of members from Reverend Ortiz and started to make disciples out of them. I was Johnny. In this new structure I am no longer needed to be a "reverend." Just Johnny. You know why? I had to be respected before. Now all I needed was love. And it's much easier to love a Johnny than to love a reverend.

So, I gave my life to these disciples. I served with

them. We went out to the country together. We lived together. We ate together. I opened my home to them. They came to sleep in my home. I went to sleep in their homes. Our wives started to meet together. We became like a family. And after six months, more or less—it didn't come overnight—these people were so changed that the whole orphanage noticed it. They stayed in the meetings. They hugged the people. They were interested in the work of the people. The people came to them for prayer, for counsel. And after six months, I allowed them to steal other members from Reverend Ortiz's church—to make disciples out of them. Six months later these, also, were allowed to steal more members. It took us almost three years, but we finally stole the whole membership and changed our orphanage into a family.

## Building the Church

In the meantime, people were being saved in small cell groups. Each one of my disciples met with his cell group. New people came into the cells, but we forbade the cell leaders to bring the new people to the church, because exposure to the old club congregation would have spoiled them. Besides, we were trying to finish off the old structure, not enlarge it. Praise the Lord, we finished. Now all are in this new structure. There were times during the transition when we made radical decisions. We shunned the building for one whole month. We just met in the homes and on Sundays went to visit Catholic churches and Baptist churches and other congregations. Each one of my disciples had a group on a different side of town, five disciples in five different spots. One of the disciples,

Gacho, worked nine hours a day repairing crashed automobiles. He had three hundred disciples under him—more than many full-time ministers. One Sunday Gacho went with all three hundred to visit a Baptist church. Can you imagine a hundred-member church with three hundred visitors! They asked, "But where are you from?"

"We are from Brother Ortiz' congregation."

"And why are you here?"

"We came to visit you."

"And your meeting?"

"We skipped church to come here."

This structure was obviously more flexible than the old one. Now we try to stay away from the building for one or two months each year. And perhaps, in the future, we will be able to do without the building entirely. Then we can put beds there, dining rooms, and help the community. The church building should not be a cave where believers hide from the world. It should be a place of service to the community. Jesus never said, "Sinners, come to the church." He said, "Believers, go ye and make disciples." Instead of sitting in our pews singing, "Come home, come home," we should sing, "Go ye, go ye. Oh seated people, go ye." How can we mobilize the dead and blind of the world if we cannot mobilize those who are alive in the congregation?

Ours, then, is a new type of church. These cells can meet in a home, in a park, in a restaurant, at the beach . . . anywhere and at any time. We have some services at six in the morning. Some cells are at midnight, because it's the only time some working people can get together. Gradually, though, we discovered what a "church member" really is.

*First,* we understood that a member is *not independent* in the body-type membership. None of us have ever seen a nose walking along the street, or a foot walking by himself. The body must be joined and fitly knitted together. If a member is independent, he is not a member. And if he is a member, he cannot be independent.

*Second,* a member is a part of the body that *unites* two other parts. The forearm unites the hand with the upper arm. A member must be united with the other two.

*Third,* a member is one who *nurtures.* He receives nourishment for himself and he passes nourishment along to other members submitted to him.

*Fourth,* a member *sustains.* The joint sustains. Would my wife ask me when I get home, "Johnny, where is your right leg?" Impossible, I cannot lose my members. They are sustained.

*Fifth,* members *pass orders.* The head makes the order to the hand, but the order is passed through the other members. The hand does not ever get offended with the forearm and say, "No, I will be detached from you. I will put a cable right from my hand to the head."

*Sixth,* this type of membership *provides elasticity to the body.* Organization is rigid. Everybody must do the same thing, sing the same way, be the same thing. People with vision, who have new ideas, new talents, have to get out of the church and into something like Campus Crusade, Youth for Christ, the Navigators, and many other extra-church organizations. But the body is elastic. And wherever there is a member of the church, there is the church. A student is going to be the church in his school. A physician is going to be the church in his office or hospital.

And from the head goes the order to the whole body, providing elasticity for the church to be the salt of the earth and the light of the world.

# CHAPTER 8

# The Need for New Wineskins

## Change of Structure in the Local Church

When we started to experience spiritual renewal in our lives and congregation through the infilling of the Spirit, we started to experience love, the fruit of the Spirit, in a deeper way. When Lordship became more real to us, we started by discipleship to form lives, to prepare workers in the bosom of the same church for the work of the ministry. Then we noticed that the structures of our church began to get in the way of this new flow of the Spirit. When we grow, things that were good for yesterday are not good for today.

I remember how proud we were when we sent our first child, David, to school. In Argentina all the school children wore white overalls. We went to the best store and bought him the most expensive overall we could find, a good strong pair. But after six months he had outgrown them and we were left with an only slightly used pair of overalls. So we had to go back to the store and buy another pair.

Now that we have four children and we know what happens, we buy the cheapest ones in the store, because we must change the overalls every six months. Our church structures are like that—we have to change them because we outgrow them. If you can live with the same structures for years and years, it is an evidence that you are not growing. If you can sing the same songs for years and years, if you can preach the same message, if you can pray the same prayers, it means you are not growing. So structures must be changed because new wine requires new skins. The difference between old skins and new ones is not because of fashion, and old skins are not set aside because they are old. They are set aside because they become hard. The skin must be soft and elastic, because when new wine ferments, the skin must be elastic enough to enlarge. In time the old skins get hard like stone, and if you put new wine in them it breaks the skin.

So it's elasticity that we need when new revelation comes, when new things are experienced. The problem can be summed up in one word: tradition.

## The Bible versus Tradition

Tradition is more firmly rooted in us than even the Word of God. We would be able to leave a verse out but unable to leave out our traditions. Many times we do things against the Bible because our actions are based on our traditions.

I remember once asking a Catholic friend, "Where do you find in the Bible the worship of Mary?"

He said, "Well, it is possible our church puts too much emphasis on Mary. But at least there is a Mary in the Bible, is there not?"

I said yes.

"But where in the Bible are the denominations that you so much defend?"

I quickly changed the subject because denominations

are a cherished Protestant tradition. Yet there is nothing about them in the Bible. To justify the silence of the Bible we tell the people that in a mysterious way, denominations are the way of God. Thus we make God guilty for our divisions, for our lack of love. And we say that Catholics are wrong because they have traditions. Of course, it's possible that the Catholic church may be wrong in places because of their traditions, but at least their traditions are older than ours. And we should be humble enough not to try to take the splinter from the eye of the Catholic brethren until we take the log out of our own. I almost wrote a book at the beginning of this renewal. It was going to be called *The Holy Traditions of the Protestant Church.* But I decided I could not do it in love, so I quit.

Where, for instance, is the verse in the Bible that says we have to pray with the eyes closed? It's as if there were a verse in the Bible that said, "And be careful, don't forget to close your eyes when you pray." On the contrary, we learn from the Bible that Jesus, in the highest prayer that He ever prayed, lifted his eyes unto heaven and said, "Father, the hour has come." He was looking. He was seeing. There is not one mention of it in the Bible, but our tradition says, *close your eyes.*

Some of our traditions nullify and oppose the Word of God. Consider baptism. The Bible says, "He that believeth and is baptized shall be saved." Our tradition says, "He that believeth is saved, and after a month of trial he will be baptized."

The Bible says, "Go and make disciples of all nations, baptizing them in the name of the Father and of the Son and of the Holy Ghost, and teaching them to observe all things." Our tradition says, "Go and make disciples, teaching them to observe all the things I have commanded you, and then baptize them." It's just the opposite. But we fight for our traditions.

"Well, I don't care what the Bible says," we proclaim angrily, "no person can join our church until the other members vote him in." Just like the club. Where did we get that? In the holy Protestant tradition perhaps. Traditions are so strong that usually when churches oust people it's not because of some doctrine of the Bible that was violated, but because they transgressed some tradition.

Oh, the power of traditions! I sometimes think that traditions have an evil spirit behind them, because they are so strong. We even see traditions in the apostles, like Peter, and God had to force him to break the tradition. Cornelius, a heathen, had received a revelation from God. God had sent an angel to him and told him to send someone to bring Peter to his house. But Peter was not like Cornelius. Peter was a man of God. He had heard Jesus Himself say to them, "Go to all the world and preach the Gospel to all creation." He had been there when Jesus said, "And you will go to Judea and to Samaria and to the uttermost part of the earth." He had also heard Jesus say, "This gospel of the kingdom shall be preached to all nations, and then the end will come." He had heard "all nations, all creatures, Jerusalem, Judea, Samaria, and to all the earth." But he would never go to preach to a person that was not a Jew—never, never, never! So when God wanted to save some Gentiles, He had to show Peter a vision of unclean animals coming from heaven. "Rise, Peter, kill and eat," the Lord said.

Peter was aghast. "Lord, no. I have never eaten such things as this and I never will!"

"Listen, Peter, don't call common and unclean what I've cleansed." The second time: "Peter, come on, kill and eat."

"Lord, no!"

Again, "What I have cleansed, don't call unclean." Once more, "Peter, kill and eat."

"Lord, no!"

Traditions are often more powerful than the actual voice of God. Who can measure the mysterious power of tradition?

If it happened to Peter, what could happen to you and to me? It's simply the power of tradition.

"No, no—God wants the denominations like they are."

"But listen, He says that He wants us to be one."

"No!"

"But the gifts. . . ."

"No!"

"But it's written. . . ."

"No!"

Our whole being says no to God when He doesn't agree with our traditions, even though we say the Bible is our only rule of faith and doctrine.

The Lord finally got through to Peter. "Three men are looking for you. You go with them, and don't doubt because I have sent them." So Peter went with the men. They told him that Cornelius was a pious man who while praying and fasting had received a vision. An angel told him to go to a certain house in a certain city, and there find a person called Peter. But when Peter got to the house, look what kind of greeting he gave to the house. He said, "You know that it is an abomination for people like us to come to see people like you." Suppose somebody came to your house and greeted you in that way. What would you say? You would say, "Listen, sir, there's the door." You can imagine what a time Cornelius faced. He had invited all his friends and told them, "You are going to hear a man of God. He must be a holy, perfect man, because the angel told me to call for him. He's going to be here any moment." Then enters tradition-bound Peter who immediately assaults everyone's sensibilities with talk of abominations. Cornelius was a gracious and humble man, and knelt down before him.

Peter, still arrogant, continued, "Well, Cornelius," he said, "God showed me that I should not be a respecter of persons, so I came. Now, what is the reason that you have called me?" An apostle of Jesus Christ did not know what to do there. Any one of us would know. Peter must have known what to say. He was the Apostle Peter. He had the gift of revelation. He had everything. Yet he said, "What is the reason that you called me?" He was doing everything he could to keep from giving the message. Why? Tradition!

They explained to him all over again. And finally Peter started to preach. But I am sure that though Peter was going to preach, he never could have given a call to the people. Peter would have preached and then gone home. That is the reason God broke through while he was still preaching. The Spirit fell over all the people and they started to praise the Lord, and to speak in tongues, and prophesy. They were shouting and singing and speaking in tongues, full of joy. Cornelius said, "Oh wife, I love you more," and he spoke in tongues. But while the people were rejoicing, Peter had a big problem. He and his Jewish companions had a board meeting in the other room.

"But, Peter, what have you done?"

"Listen, I didn't baptize them in the Spirit—it was God. I couldn't help what happened."

"Well, what are we going to do? Shall we baptize them? What a problem!"

The other people had no problem. They were full of joy. But the traditionalists had a tremendous problem. They didn't know what to do with the blessing of God.

"Well, what shall we do?" says Peter.

"I think we should baptize them. Because if God gave them. . . ."

"Well, if you baptize them, Peter, that's up to you. We wash our hands of this."

Traditions, how strong they are!

When they went back to their church the disciples of Peter had heard the news already. They were waiting for Peter with one stone in each hand. Peter arrived. "Hello, praise the Lord, brothers."

"At six o'clock a board meeting."

"What?"

"At six o'clock a board meeting."

"But, listen."

"No, we are going to talk after the meeting."

When they got to the meeting, the elders of the church said, "We heard that you went to a Gentile house and that you ate with them! Is that true?" They were scandalized. They said it must be the devil because they were not accustomed to it. Then Peter told the story all over again. "And while I was preaching the Holy Spirit came."

"No!"

"Yes, and they spoke in tongues."

"No!"

"Yes! So what could I do but baptize them? I couldn't withhold baptism because the same thing that happened to us at Pentecost happened to them."

Then the people said, "So also to the Gentiles God gives forgiveness! Well, praise the Lord!"

If this happened to the Apostle Peter, what could happen to us? I am bound by tradition. I'm preaching these things and yet every day I follow tradition in many things. It is very difficult to get free from tradition. Sometimes I think that no one of us is going to enter the new thing God is doing in this day. Because we come from Egypt, we are unused to the promised land, and may need to die in the wilderness; perhaps our sons must also. Then, free of tradition, our grandchildren can enter into the thing that God is doing in these last days.

I was once a member of a very sophisticated church. One day I went to a Pentecostal church and they were clapping their hands in the meeting. I said, "Ohhhhh! these are worldly people, they are clapping their hands!" My mind couldn't bear that. When I shared my views with them, they said, "No, brother, listen. In the Psalms we read of clapping the hands." But still I had problems.

Then once God came with power in a meeting and all the people started to dance with joy. "Ohhhhh—what's this? It's a new doctrine. No, no. I won't allow this!" Somebody came to me and said, "There is a verse, *'Dance unto the Lord.'* "

"It's a verse? But I am not accustomed to this unclean thing."

"What I have cleansed, you do not call unclean."

"But Lord, no."

"Listen, what I have cleansed. . . ."

"No! no!"

Oh, traditions, traditions! Our minds are so conditioned. Let's see if we can enlarge our minds a little bit, because God is doing something new, and we are going to miss it if our minds stay small.

A woman broke a bottle of perfume and poured it over the head of Jesus. It was something of the Spirit. The disciples were scandalized. "Look what she did! We could have sold that for so much money and given it to the poor!" Jesus said, "She has done a good thing." Traditions were very, very strong even with the apostles. God wants to do greater things but He can't because of us; He promised not to give us more than we could bear. But wouldn't it be nice if we could bear it when the Lord wanted to give us something new?

## Qualifications for Renewal

Paul said in Romans 12, "I urge you therefore, brethren, by the mercies of God, to present your bodies a living and holy sacrifice, acceptable to God, which is your spiritual service of worship. And do not be conformed to this world, but be transformed by the renewing of your mind, that you may prove what the will of God is, that which is good and acceptable and perfect." To experience the will of God we must meet two qualifications.

*First,* our body must be in complete surrender to Him

as a living sacrifice. A living sacrifice is better than a dead one. Because with the dead sacrifice, God must accept it dead. But with a living sacrifice, God can do whatever He wants. It's more in His hands. Thus we must present ourselves as a living sacrifice to experience His will.

*Second,* we must be ready to be transformed, to be changed by the renewing of our mind. Then we will *stay* in the will of God. Sometimes we say, "Lord, show us thy will." It's the same thing as if a train would say, "Please give me a steering wheel." Who needs a steering wheel when there are tracks? Our traditions are our tracks, our structures. We pray, piously, "God, show us thy will," but the tracks are already made.

We are like the car on the merry-go-round that is attached to the platform. It has a steering wheel and the child turns it one way and then the other, but the car always remains stationary. That's how we are in our churches. We are attached to the platform of our traditions. Yet we say, "God, show me thy will."

So, in order to experience the will of God, we need to give our whole lives as a living sacrifice. That means we detach our little cars from their merry-go-round platforms and let God take us for a real ride.

In our situation we began to discover the structures of our church were a hindrance more than a help to acceptance of this new wine that God was giving us. The need for change was obvious. Praise the Lord, the people were ready.

Democracy seems a necessary evil in most churches, and we had a very democratic church. The primitive church was not a democratic institution—it was theocratic. God, the head, commanded. The apostles received the signs from the Lord and told the people what the Lord told them. The early church was commanded by the Lord, the head—not by the feet. Under the Head were the apostles. Under the apostles were the disciples. The power came from above, working downward. In our democratic system, however, the power is in the base, the feet, not in the head. The head must obey the orders of the feet.

In the beginning the church never sought for volunteers. Paul didn't say, "Is there anyone who will volunteer to come with me and help?" He said, "You, Timothy! You come with me!" It was a revelation of God.

The apostles even defined the doctrine. As a matter of fact, the Acts report that the people followed the doctrine of the apostles—not the doctrine of Jesus, but the doctrine of the apostles. The things they wrote were infallible—a concept we still believe. They believed the apostles were led by the Holy Spirit in founding the church.

But after some years the church lost its charisma, its spiritual power. The leaders became materialistic. They were more conscious of earthly power than the power that came from above. The church stayed with the same type of government, but began to doubt the Spirit. So while the type of government was orthodox, the power was gone. The Catholic church is that type of church. When the pope says that he is infallible, he is not too far from the truth. He reasons, "If Paul wrote a letter it was infallible because he was an apostle. If John wrote a letter it was infallible because he was an apostle. If Peter wrote a letter it was infallible because he was an apostle. I am an apostle also because I am a descendant of Peter. How can I write a letter and it not be infallible?" That's not bad logic.

However, without the charismata, without the immediate and pervasive activity of the Holy Spirit, the church became a danger to the world. Without God's revelation the church started to go astray. Some of the sons of the church, like Savonarola, Wycliffe, Huss, and others were persecuted and killed because the church was bound in tradition that made it largely deaf to the voice of God. If the church had had revelation, the church would have admitted and accepted those ministries. The church would have been renewed by those people and the story of the world would have been different. The Catholic church admits that if Luther were living today they would not excommunicate him. They would instead be enriched by that new life that God was giving to the church. But in the sixteenth century they did excommunicate him. That was the problem of having the correct government without revelation.

## Church Government

The Protestant Reformation was, in many ways, a reaction to that problem. The result was the democratic church. This was good at the beginning. It brought to the people the consciousness that they had to vote, they had to think, they had to work. The so-called laymen became more engaged in the work of the church. For a time it was better, but it was not the cure. In the Dark Ages the Pope substituted for the Word of God. But in the Protestant church, the Word of God was substituted by the voice of the majority. So it was not a cure because men were still in control. The people couldn't say, "God said." They said, "Let's vote on it. If it comes to more than half, let's think we have the will of God." But the majority is not always right. It was the majority that made the golden calf in the wilderness. The majority left Jesus to go alone to the cross. So we cannot say that something is right because the majority votes for it. Yet today we still equate the vote of the people with the voice of God.

If the ministries and charismata are restored, they will bring an end to democracy. I am not for an episcopal government without charisma and revelation, but neither do I favor a democratic government because it is not biblical. Both things are going to end when God brings charisma. Perhaps the churches with bishops will be more ready—I don't say more open—but maybe it will be easier for them to accept.

The concept of episcopal authority is biblical. I invited a Catholic priest to preach in my church. He first asked permission of his bishop. The bishop said, "You may go, but don't take anybody with you except the most spiritually mature people of your parish." He had previously promised to come with all the parish. But when he arrived, he apologized, saying, "I'm sorry. I came with only three people because the bishop told me not to bring those who are not spiritually grounded." So perhaps they are more ready than we—the democratic people—to be submissive.

We are not yet ready to solve the problem of which is the best form of government for the church. How can we have a biblical form of government in a nonbiblical church? In the Bible we find the church in only two dimensions: the universal or catholic church, and the local church. The universal church is the church of the whole earth. And the local church is the church at a certain locality. All the local churches together form the universal church. It is very easy to put a biblical type of government into this type of church.

The problem is that in recent centuries a new type of church has appeared, a church that is neither universal nor local. It's bigger than local, and smaller than universal. It is the denomination. The denominations have tried every form of government, from the episcopal system on the right to the congregational system on the left, with presbyterianism in the middle. Each system had some biblical precedent. The problem lies in the fact that there is no biblical precedent for denominationalism. Any form, no matter how biblical, is bound to fail in the framework of denominationalism. So long as we cling to the old wineskins of our denominations, we will not move ahead with God.

I saw this principle illustrated while I was in Ecuador. There I saw big sweet bananas. I said, "I've never seen such bananas as these in my country. Ours are small. Could I take a plant of these big bananas to my country?"

But somebody explained, "In order to have these bananas in your country you must take not only the plant, you must take the soil, the rain, the temperature—you must take the whole equatorial atmosphere to your country. If you take this plant to your country, you are going to have small bananas, because in your country it is cold. Even if you take the biggest banana plant, you will still have small bananas."

When we receive the baptism of the Spirit, we say, "Oh, this is the key." Immediately we want to take the dimension of the Spirit back into our denominational structure just as I wanted to take an Ecuadorian banana

plant back to Argentina. But the task is impossible. The
Holy Spirit of today is the same Spirit that was in the
primitive church. And He will not function properly in
the cold climate of denominationalism. You cannot have
equatorial bananas in Argentina where it is cold. We have
to bring the whole equator.

Then, we cannot have the full power of the Holy
Spirit in today's church because it is not an equator
church, the church as it was in the beginning. Remember,
in every locality there is only one church. Jesus has only
one wife. He's not a polygamist. He has one church. We
cannot make two churches, because it is one by nature.

Recently I was in the city of Charlotte, North
Carolina. I was told there are four hundred churches in
that city. That is not true. There is one church broken into
four hundred pieces. So we should find out how to put the
pieces together, because there cannot be more than one
church in each locality. If we have here a church, and
there another church, which of these is the local church?
There cannot be more than one church in any locality. So
in a given city there are not ten churches, but one church.
You should go to the top of the highest building of your
city and say, "Lord, show me the church in this city as
You see it." We may think that God is looking from
heaven through a tube connected to our church saying,
"What nice people. How nicely they sing. What a nice
organ they bought. What a nice carpet they put in the
building."

But in truth He is weeping, as Jesus wept over
Jerusalem. He says, "How many times I was willing to
gather your children as a hen gathers her chicks, but you
wouldn't let me." So ask the Lord to give you the vision of

the church of the city as He sees it—one church all divided into pieces.

## Pastors and Elders

This raises the question: Who are the pastors in a city like Charlotte? To begin with, there are no pastors of the churches of Charlotte, rather there are pastors of *the church* of Charlotte. Now if they are the pastors of the same church, they are actually co-pastors. If they are co-pastors, they should have fellowship. They should meet. They should love one another. They should share together. They should almost live together. Even if the one church is scattered, the pastors stick together, because the Head, Jesus Christ, sends His light to the community of ministers. We need apostles and prophets and teachers and evangelists and pastors for the perfecting of the saints.

So in the plural ministry each pastor is an elder of the church of his city. Together they form the presbytery, the assembly of elders of the city. We are wrong when we appoint elders within our separate congregations. We cannot have elders within each congregation. Each part of the flock will have only *one* shepherd. One of the elders of the city will live with that group. That Methodist or Baptist congregation is just a part of *the church* supervised by one of the elders of the city. We had appointed elders in our congregation. But when I became one of the elders of the city, my elders became the helpers of one of the elders of the city. Everyone was lowered one degree. Before I was the pastor of the local church, then I became one of the elders of the local church. And the elders of this local church became the helpers of one of the elders of the local church, the local church being comprised of all the believers in the city. In every city there should be a similar presbytery. Jesus, who walks among the candlesticks, is the Head of all the local churches that are under Him. Of course, the local churches meet their situation: the Jerusalem church was different from the Antioch church, but they were local churches. And through the apostles the whole church got together under the lordship of Jesus Christ. So there's a change that needs to come in the structure of the local church. Stay in your churches; be as faithful as you can. But don't forget that you must be part of the city church.

# CHAPTER 9

# Koinonia and Community Living

## How to Make Disciples

One of the most controversial and misunderstood teachings of the Bible is how to make disciples. I'm always hesitant when asked to explain this concept, because it can be construed as mechanics. People can be tempted to copy it. And if you put this thing into practice without the renewal of the whole congregation you are going to become frustrated. I am going to talk in terms of mechanics in this chapter because this is a deductive teaching situation. But in real life, concepts are not born from copying mechanics; they emerge from experiences. Often we'll find ourselves practicing the right methods without being able to frame them in proper terminology.

Now I can look back at the picture and describe what happened in our midst. First came the reality of the lordship of Christ and His love, and our methods for making disciples were consequences of that. That was the wine and we had to provide a new wineskin for it. There is no need for a new wineskin if there is no new wine. Most important is the wine—then comes the new wineskin. So in this chapter I want to share something about the new wineskin.

Discipleship starts with pastors. If the pastors don't get together to disciple themselves first, they will never be able to make disciples out of other people. To make disciples we must be disciples. Discipleship is not just teaching the Bible as we used to teach it. Discipleship is a life relationship, not a classroom situation. You cannot take old sermons and teach them to new disciples. To make disciples, you need to have the Word of God for today, as well as Bible study.

The Word and the will of God for our lives today should come first to the group of pastors that get together in a certain city. When the pastors meet together and minister to the Lord (waiting and praying in love) God reveals to them the purpose for the city and His purpose for the disciples. The Bible will help in discipleship. But the living Word of God, the will of God for today, is what really makes disciples. Thus it is needful for the pastors to come together. If the pastors are not submissive one to another, how can they have people submissive under them? The pastor might rebuke his disciples when they are wrong, but who rebukes him when he is wrong? He corrects them if they are wrong, but who corrects him if he is wrong? The only guarantee the disciples have when they submit to an elder is that he is part of the presbytery of that city.

Pastors become disciples so they can make disciples. As a proud Pentecostal I thought I had everything because I belonged to a Full Gospel church. Little did I know how much I had to learn until I came together with other pastors—Baptists, Presbyterians, Plymouth Brethren, and Catholics. As a proud Pentecostal I had to become a humble elder of the church.

After the mother cell began to function, the pastors then had to choose their disciples. This choosing must not be for personal effect, nor for the education of the people. The choosing of the disciple had to come by pure guidance from God. Paul chose Timothy. According to the flesh, I would never have chosen Timothy, because he was too young and too shy. And at first he was continually ill. I would never choose a weak, shy, and too-young disciple. But Paul did because he was listening to God.

It wasn't Timothy who wanted to go with Paul, rather Paul who wanted Timothy to go with him. So he was chosen by the guidance of God. Jesus prayed forty days before choosing His twelve disciples. He knew the choosing of the disciples had to be made in prayer.

Although most of the men chosen as disciples in our church worked in offices and factories during the day, they still had seven nights a week for meetings. One night was spent meeting with the one to whom they submitted, another night for meeting with the ones who submitted to them. Every disciple had responsibility over two types of cells, one cell where he formed the lives of the new converts, and another cell where he took the most advanced of those new converts and taught them how to be leaders, knowing that cell would soon be divided and the most advanced disciples put over additional cells. So came the multiplication. There was a "formation of life" cell, and a "formation of leader" cell. Each disciple attended two cell meetings in addition to the cell where he received for himself.

The fourth night of the seven was used for a group meeting of all disciples. Usually this was on Sunday. If they were married, one night was reserved for the family.

Those who were single were required to give a night to their parents simply because people teach by the lives they live, not by the way they talk.

Since most of the cell meetings lasted four to six hours, one night was set aside for rest. Like the meetings, rest time was not a suggestion, it was a commandment. Disciples must rest for the kingdom's sake, because the Lord needs them fresh to do His work. Sunday, as we know it, is not a day of rest. It is the day we get most tired. We get up early to go to Sunday school. Then we have the morning service, the young people, finally the evening service, followed by a fellowship meeting. When God said, "Rest!" He meant rest! The people who make clothes put labels in them which explain proper care and cleaning of the clothes. So when God made our bodies, He said, "One day in seven this machine has to rest." So we commanded the disciples to rest.

The last night of the week was used for the disciple to bring out any needs that he might have. Sometimes this was used for a special meeting with their elders. Other times one of their disciples might need to come to them with a special problem. Or perhaps the night was used for chores around the house.

Such a vigorous routine demanded we discontinue the meeting on Sunday morning. Our people needed to sleep Sunday morning because they were working so hard during the week. So we commanded the people to stay home and sleep until ten or eleven o'clock on Sunday. It was a radical departure from tradition, but it got results.

Once a month we had a weekend for all the cells to be together. Each cell did the same thing. Beginning on

Friday night and lasting through Sunday lunch, we all got together to share, to confess our sins to one another, to make the community relationship easier, or to be alone in the country, living together.

Of course, in order to live like this, the person must be completely committed to the kingdom of God. Even though each man was working, he spent his time thinking of what he would be doing after the work time, and how he could better use his work time for God's glory. All twenty-four hours of the day were committed to the kingdom. That's discipleship.

## What Is a Cell? A Community?

"Cell" is a transitory name we used for a meeting of five or more persons for certain purposes. I say it is a transitory name because we don't see the word "cell" in the Bible. The proper name should be "church in the home." But the name "church in the home" brings to mind the type of church we used to have. So we use the word "cell" to show it is not a common meeting where they go to a home, open the Bible, read and discuss it, sing a chorus, then pray and go home. That's no advantage— that's the same as we always did. Therefore we called our new meetings "cells" because they were a completely different concept.

New people were brought into a cell for a year's time and taught to function as members of the kingdom. Next they graduated into a "small community" where we emphasized sharing and community love. In the community people learned the real meaning of living together as

kingdom people. The early church practiced koinonia, and
we learned we could not be kingdom people unless we
practiced it also.

We sought to put an end to poverty in our congregation. If we could not bring social justice to our own
congregation, with people who had Bibles under their
arms, we could never bring it to others. Social justice had
to start within our congregation—the household of faith.
This meant it was unthinkable for one brother to have two
TV sets while another brother didn't even have a bed to
sleep in. It was unthinkable for one person to have three
cars, while another person had to walk twenty blocks to
catch a bus. We knew that only when we became living
examples could we go with authority to the world and tell
them about social justice. First we had to clean our own
house. This is what "community" is all about.

We were careful not to give any title to the cell leader.
Titles corrupt. We stopped laying hands on people to
"ordain" them to a ministry with a title. We used to lay
hands on anyone and everyone. But I found that I myself,
the ordained minister, was not even qualified to be a
deacon in the primitive church. A deacon in the primitive
church had more spirituality, more wisdom, more power,
more gifts, than the most reverend minister of today. Thus
I dropped my "Reverend" title. If I did everything God
commanded, the only diploma I was fit to receive would
be inscribed "unprofitable servant." And I'm not even an
unprofitable servant yet. Authority comes by spirituality,
not by titles. If a person grows spiritually, even though he
does not have the title of "elder," other people will submit
to him. But if a person lacks that anointing of unfeigned
spirituality, even the title "The Most Reverend" won't

make up for it. This does not mean titles are wrong. It does mean, however, we should be more careful and let God choose the elders. After God sets them in the body and they are functioning, there is plenty of time to recognize it by giving them titles.

Cells can meet anywhere. If it is too hot in the living room, they can meet on the beach or in the park. They can meet any time. Some of our cells met at six in the morning because the men worked at night. Some met at 2 A.M. It was quite different from church at eleven o'clock on Sunday only.

## A Group and a Task

I used to be a task-minded pastor. I used people as tools to achieve my aspirations. But persons are not objects to be used by somebody else. A spiritual leader is not a company executive who sees the employees as tools to meet his ends. Our cell leaders had to realize that each one of these people was a disciple. Each of them had needs—social needs, spiritual needs, material needs—and had his own aspirations in life. The leader had to develop a sensitivity to the peculiar personalities and needs of the people who comprised his cell.

As a young evangelist I used to go into the country and preach to little churches in small towns. I was a nobody. When I visited the central office of my denomination no one said to me, "Hello," "Good morning," "Good afternoon." I went in, sat down, and went out—that was all. But when I became pastor of a big city church, things changed. Then when I visited the central office or the Bible School, people fawned over me. "Oh, Brother Ortiz, hello. Give me your coat. Do you want a cup of tea?" But I knew if I moved back to the small churches I would become a nobody once again. We use people. If we bring money, if we build up more churches, if we multiply—ohhhh! But if we fall in disgrace, who takes care of us?

Now God has revealed to us a new dimension of the kingdom. We love people. We want to bring them into a group where their needs will be met. They come to the group not because we call them ("Don't forget to come. Please come! Promise me that you will come."). No, they come because they cannot help coming, because here they find a new kind of love. They become part of a caring family moving in the Holy Spirit. This family is sensitive to and can help supply their social, material, and spiritual needs. They become brothers and sisters in a family of love. And the group thrives as its inner life—the caring for one another—is balanced with its outer life—the task. The task is the great commission of our Lord Jesus Christ. This group is made-to-order to fulfill the task, to make disciples of all nations. The group would become a swampy pool without the thrust provided by its task. So both things are very important, the loving group—and the task.

## Elements of a Cell

A cell has five elements: 1) devotion; 2) discussion; 3) programming; 4) mobilization; 5) multiplication. It takes all five to form a cell group. This does not mean that all five will be present every time the cell meets. Perhaps one week will be all devotions, another week could be all discussion. But in the ongoing life of the cell, these five elements must be present. In Acts 19, when Paul made disciples and they filled the whole province of Asia with the gospel, they had devotions and discussion, they programmed where they were going to go, they mobilized the people to go to different cities, and they multiplied. They founded many churches in that province.

Devotions entail prayer, worship, praise, confession, and breaking. Through these the group transacts with God, and to them it must always resort because the group's life depends utterly on God.

Discussion is the milk of the Word. We don't give lessons as we used to, once a week. Now one lesson from the Word lasts many months. We don't pass on to the next lesson until we are practicing the previous one. The Bible says it is the doers of the Word who shall be justified, not the hearers of the Word. Why are there so many hearers? Because there are so many speakers. If we speak, and speak, and speak, what can people do but hear? Studies show that audiences remember only one-fifth, or twenty percent, of the things they hear in a sermon. If they don't practice it, in ten days they forget even that fifth. They might even hear another message in the meantime that divides their attention. What do we remember from our school days? We remember how to write, how to read, how to add, subtract, multiply, and perhaps how to divide. But we don't remember the story of China or the geography of India, because we didn't practice those things. We remember the things we kept on practicing. It is the same way with the things of God. Jesus didn't say, "Teach them to *know* all the things that I commanded you," but "Teach them to *observe* all the things I have commanded you." Therefore discussion means not only giving lessons that they might hear, but also putting them into practice.

We used to have a prayer meeting on Tuesday, so I would frequently speak about prayer. "Prayer changes things. Prayer is the most important thing. Pray, pray." The people agreed. They went home thinking that prayer was so important. Then they came back the next Tuesday, and I would give them a bible study on the book of Nehemiah, the walls of Jerusalem, the doors and the rebuilding of the walls. "What a man, Nehemiah. We need people like Nehemiah today." In a few weeks I would speak on prayer again but we never did get around to prayer itself.

On Sunday they came back to church. In Sunday school they studied about the tabernacle, the courts, and the holy place. Ah, the tabernacle, that's something really important. But talking about prayer, Nehemiah, and the tabernacle in rapid succession so divided their attention that they actually absorbed very little. After the tabernacle, they went to the worship service and heard a message about holiness unto the Lord. God wants holiness, because without holiness nobody can please God. Forget about the tabernacle, Nehemiah, prayer—holiness is the thing. Then they came to the night service and heard "The Lord is coming soon. Because He is coming we must prepare. . . ." Ah, the second coming, yes. Forget about prayer, Nehemiah, the tabernacle, holiness, now it is the second coming. And so on for years and years. What can people do but hear? Five messages a week. Two hundred sixty messages in a year. Whew! Now we have only four or five messages a year. We started discipleship three years ago and are on the eleventh lesson. But the church is completely changed—because we are practicing it.

## Teaching Sound Doctrine

The cell groups are used to teach sound doctrine. In Titus we learn that this means, among other things, that the older women teach the younger ones how to behave in their homes—how to be submissive to their husbands, how to be sensible, pure, workers at home, and how to train their children. If an older woman has sound doctrine she should be teaching the younger ones.

Sound doctrine is not just belief in the millennium, the rapture, and the tribulation. Those are the philosophical definitions of our belief. Sound doctrine is teaching an employee not to be argumentative with his employer. Many deacons in churches today feel they are good deacons because they signed the articles of faith. They believe in the resurrection of the dead, the coming of the Lord, the new birth, and water baptism. Yet they are argumentative in their work. They do not have sound doctrine. If a believer is on the highway and sees a sign saying "60 miles per hour maximum speed," and he goes to 80, he is disobedient to authority. He lacks sound doctrine. "Well, he believes in the millennium." I don't care what he believes about that—the speed of his car tells me more about his doctrine than does the cast of his millennialism.

"Husbands, love your wives as Jesus loved the church. Don't be rough with them. Honor them as the weaker vessel." That is sound doctrine. We have deacons in all churches who don't love their wives. They are rough with them. They don't treat them as weaker vessels. But they believe in the millennium. They believe in the tribulation. They even believe in angels and archangels, but they are fooling themselves, because sound doctrine means a husband must love his wife.

"Wives, be submissive to your husbands." Some churches have deaconesses who are the heads of the houses. They believe in the millennium, but they don't submit to their husbands.

"Children, be obedient. Submit to your parents." We have Sunday school teachers who are disobedient to their parents. They agree with the articles of faith of the denomination, but they don't have sound doctrine. Sound doctrine is not the formula of the beliefs of our denomination; it is our conduct, the life we live. Jesus said, "Teach them to observe all the things that I have commanded you." That is really sound doctrine.

So, in these cells we give the disciples milk—sound doctrine. The first principles of the gospel—repentance, faith, baptism—are not even the milk yet. The first water the mother gives her child purges him. Then comes the milk. Faith, repentance, baptism, burdens in the spirit—all those things are the purgative. Then, and only then, do we come to the precious holy Scriptures, the milk of the Word of God.

So in the first session of a cell group, for instance, we discuss the lesson material on husbands. The second week we review the material by questions and answers to be sure everybody understands what a husband is and how a husband should act. The third week we take the first point in our lesson on husbands: the husband is the head of the

wife and of the home. The second point is: the husband
must love the wife. The third point: the husband must
provide for the home. On the third week, when we start
with the first point, we discuss how to put it into practice
with each person we have in the cell. Suppose we have in
the cell Peter, Johnny, and several others. We ask Peter if
he is really the head of his house. Peter answers, "Well,
brother, you know when we went through this, I had a big
problem. I now realize that I am not the head of my home,
because I don't know how to solve the problems. It
happened that my father-in-law died. He had a big dog
that he loved very much. The dog reminded my mother-in-
law of my father-in-law. I had to bring my mother-in-law
to my home to live with us, and she of course brought the
dog. We live in a small apartment which is inadequate for
the dog. I began to quarrel with my wife and my
mother-in-law. I said the dog should get out.

"My wife said, 'But poor Mom, she is so old. The dog
reminds her of Daddy. Be kind. Don't put the dog out.'

"I replied, 'The dog *must* get out of the house.'

"Every day we had a fight. The situation got so bad
that I didn't know whether I really loved my wife. It is still
the same. Perhaps we will have to get a divorce."

Another person says, "Listen, Peter, I can help you. I
live out on the outskirts of the city in a home with a large
piece of land. You can give me the dog and I will take care
of it."

Another says, "No, Peter, perhaps God sent the dog
to your home to teach you something. Because you are not
the head of your house. Because a head is not only to
command everybody, he is to bring solutions, to think
things out. You have a situation in your family, and you as

head cannot solve that situation. How can it be that a dog
can make more trouble than you? How can it be that a
dog is more important than you? He is undoing all the
family. You are not a dog, you are a person."

Another says, "Listen, Peter, of course we think that a
dog shouldn't be in an apartment, but perhaps God wants
to teach you a lesson. Why don't you try to love that dog?
You are losing your wife and that poor old woman is
heartbroken. You are the problem, not the dog."

"Oh, but I cannot. Don't tell me that a dog is for an
apartment."

"Don't worry. We are going to pray that God gives
you power to accept that dog. Come on, sit down here
please."

We all gather around him. We lay hands on him and
pray for him, "God, give him victory over the dog. Give
him love for his wife, love for the mother-in-law. Help
him."

Peter starts to weep and says, "I've got the victory."

"Now, first thing when you go home, buy a new collar
for the dog."

"I'll do it."

"If you have no money, we can give you some to buy
a nice one, because you must love the dog."

While all this is going on, my wife is with Peter's wife
in another cell. Peter's wife tells about the problem of the
dog and the husband and the poor mama. My wife tells
Peter's wife, "Listen, he is the head of the house and you
and your mother should submit to him. If he says that the
dog must be out, you should obey. The dog must be out of
the house. Why don't you take the dog to some friend's
house and you can visit the dog once or twice a week.

Obey your husband. He is the head. And your mother must obey him also, because now he is her head too."

"I never thought about it that way. I'll discuss it with Mama."

Mama and daughter decided to give the dog away. And the same day Peter comes home with a new collar for the dog!

When we finish with Peter, we start with Johnny. When we finish with Johnny, we start with one of the others. The following week they come with their testimonies: "Do you know what happened? The dog is no longer at our house. It's sad, because I really started to love that dog." Everybody brings his testimony. That is why the cell meetings last four or five or six hours with only five people. We no longer have time for Sunday morning services. We're too busy learning sound doctrine to listen to sermons about Nehemiah.

We may spend two weeks on the first point. Then comes the second point—to love your wife. Here comes the mystical part of matrimony. A man who has never given his wife flowers now starts to do it. Roses, and a box of candy. And the transformation begins.

The third point is to provide. Maybe someone in the cell group says, "We are in need, we haven't enough money."

"How much do you earn?"

"$200 a month."

"How many do you have in the family?"

"Four."

"Oh, I earn $400 and I have six children; it's enough for me."

"Come on, tell us, how do you do it?"

"Well, we buy at such-and-such a market. We also buy with our neighbors. A whole sack of potatoes is cheaper than buying by the dozen. Then we divide." In our cells we may speak of heaven and seraphs, but we also speak about the cost of living, about politics, because we are integrated persons. We are not just *souls*. We are *soul* and *body* and *spirit*. In the kingdom of God there is no such thing as a spiritual gospel and a social gospel. It is the gospel of the kingdom. It is a whole package.

After two or three months we have finished one lesson. But all the homes are completely changed. The difference: they are not hearers, but doers of the Word.

The cells, then, make up the skeleton of the church. The Sunday night meeting is the skin and the beauty of the church. In the cells we nourish the strength of the church. In the Sunday meeting we find the mystical. Some people have nice skin, but no skeleton. We have a sturdy skeleton with a healthy covering of meat and skin.

In this kind of relationship, submission is very important. A rebellious spirit will destroy the body. Submission proves whether a person is really broken. Brokenness is not just tears; it is obedience. You can fill many handkerchiefs at every meeting and not be broken. If you have to weep a great deal it shows you are not getting broken. In brokenness you don't have to weep. You just obey. Submission, of course, is by love. Take love out of matrimony, and the wife becomes a slave who cooks and cleans just for the roof, clothing, and food. But put in love and the slave becomes a wife. Submission is a thing of love.

# CHAPTER 10

# Three Degrees of Love: The Old Commandment

> A new commandment I give unto you, that you love
> one another; as I have loved you, that ye also love one
> another. By this shall all men know that ye are my
> disciples, if ye love one another (John 13:34, 35).

Love is the most important virtue of the Christian life.
Love, says the Apostle Paul, endures forever. Tongues,
prophecies, signs, everything else is going to pass away;
but love will abide forever. Love is the eternal element in
the Christian life. One who loves lives in God, and God in
him.

Usually when we speak of eternity we think in terms
of time. But what about the quality of that eternity? The
quality is *love*. Many people think they have eternal life
(meaning they will live forever), but which kind of life?
What makes this life different is the quality. In evangelistic
meetings I used to say, "Raise your hands and you will
have eternal life."

"What is eternal life?"

"It means that when you die you'll go to heaven. You
will live forever."

But it's more than that, much more. We forget the
most important thing, because even sinners are going to
have eternal life—another kind of life, but eternal in hell.

What makes the difference? Love!

You may have the gifts, you may have all the things you want, but if you don't have love, you have nothing. You may be a member of a good church, you may sing in the choir, you may have visions, dreams, and speak in tongues; but those things are not eternal. "If we walk in the light, as He is in the light, we have communion one with another, and the blood of Jesus cleanses us from all sin." What is that light in which we have to walk? John says that he who loves his brother is in the light, and he who doesn't love his brother is in the darkness. The light of God is love. To walk in the light is to walk in love.

If we don't have love, we don't have eternal life. The Bible says that he who loves his brother has passed from death to life. He who doesn't love is still in death, even if he speaks in tongues.

Satan is successful when he gets us to put emphasis on unessential things and to treat lightly the element that is really essential. I Corinthians 13 says that even the great gifts of tongues of angels and men, of prophecy, of wisdom, of knowledge, faith to move mountains—all those great and wonderful things are nothing at all if we have not the eternal element of the Christian life: love.

Love is not something to study about, it is something to live by. I may teach many things about the Christian life, about the millennium, about the tribulation, about the angels, the seraphim, Satan, the fall; but only love is alive. When a person loves, it is impossible to hide it. When I fell in love for the first time, the girl and I agreed to keep it a secret. But that night when I got home, I was so happy I was singing.

My mother asked, "What's happened to you, Johnny?"

"Nothing, Mother."

"Come on, something has happened to you."

She knew I was in love, because love is alive. I couldn't hide it. "By this," Jesus said, "shall all men know that ye are my disciples." Not if you believe in the baptism of the Holy Spirit, or if you believe the millennium comes first, only if you love one another.

Many people are always following after the gifts of the Spirit. I like the gifts. In Argentina I am called a "charismatic." But a person with the gifts of the Spirit is like a Christmas tree. A Christmas tree is wonderful on Christmas day, because it is surrounded by packages and bedecked with glittering tinsel. But if you take the packages away from the Christmas tree, the tree is rather plain. The day after Christmas all the garbage cans are full of Christmas trees, because they have begun to dry up and lose their beauty. Their presence in our homes was a fleeting and unnatural thing. Christmas trees do "bear" a kind of fruit—like watches, jewelry, clothing and candies —but that is artificial fruit. It really tells us little about the tree itself. If on the other hand you find an apple well attached to a tree, you identify it as an apple tree. To know what a person is, you have to look beneath the leaves of the tree to see what kind of fruit he has. Don't be dazzled by any tinsel you might come across in your search; it was just hung there by the Holy Ghost. Just look between the leaves to see what kind of fruit that tree has. The fruit of the Spirit is love. If that person—that tree—has love, joy, peace, patience, kindness, goodness, faithfulness, humility, self-control, then that person is a tree of God.

Be careful, don't get confused. These are days in which people must be able to discern what is of God and what is not. But you won't need special gifts of discernment and interpretation to understand this: any believer can learn to be a fruit inspector. "By this shall all men know that ye are my disciples." By what? By rising from the dead? No. By speaking in tongues? Hindus and spiritualists speak in tongues. By moving mountains? Not so. By giving to the poor? Not even that, because Paul says that we can give all our wealth to the poor, and if we lack love we are nothing. "By this shall all men know that ye are my disciples, if ye have love one to another."

I would prefer to have all those gifts and the apples too. That would be best. But love is the only eternal element of the Christian life. If I have eternal life, it is because I have love. He that loves, lives in God, and God in him.

I was a pastor for many years, and I didn't know what love was. Oh, I preached many times about love, both from the Greek and the Hebrew. I knew all the words. I could preach good sermons about love. But I didn't know what it meant. Since then experience has taught me that there are three degrees of love.

When people hear Jesus' words, "A new commandment I give unto you, that ye love one another," they say, "We know that commandment already, it's not new." But wait a moment—He said, "As I loved you, ye love one another."

The old commandment about love, "Love thy neighbor as thyself," is the minimum requirement. The least that God expects of us is that we should love our neighbor as ourselves. He doesn't say "love your brother" because love among the brothers should be a matter of much greater intensity.

The old commandment does not concern love in the church among the brethren. It is the commandment of God to all humanity. Everyone should love his neighbor as himself.

If you have a bowl of soup and your neighbor does not, you should share half of it with him. If your children are clothed and your neighbor's children are not, you should use your means to get clothes for them as well.

A lawyer once asked Jesus, "Who is my neighbor?" Do you know who your neighbor is? Perhaps you don't. For many years I lived thinking I knew who my neighbor was, and I didn't.

One night I said, "Lord, tomorrow morning I will start to love my neighbor." In the morning I said to myself, "Johnny, you must love your neighbor! But who is he?"

Our Lord answered the lawyer's and my question by telling the parable of the good Samaritan. It was a puzzling answer because after hearing it neither the lawyer nor I got a real definition of neighbor from it.

I had preached on this parable many times, but I never got what God was trying to tell me. I always spiritualized it. Jerusalem is the church; Jericho is the world; the person is the man who leaves the church; Satan, the "thief" with his demons, robs him of his spiritual things and leaves him half dead "spiritually." And the good Samaritan is the believer who says, "Please come to church again." That is *not* what Jesus meant to say. Jesus said, "You go and do the same." The parable is much easier to interpret than the way I had done it. It simply means that if a man has love in his heart and sees somebody in need, he will help him. He will not stop to ask, "Is this my neighbor?" Love does not begin by defining its objects, it discovers them. A man doesn't fail to love his neighbor because he can't decide who his neighbor is, but because his heart is empty of love in the first place.

Our title for the parable is the "good" Samaritan. Jesus did not say he was "good," just that he was a Samaritan. We call a person who fulfills the old commandment "good." But in Jesus' parable he was just a man who had in his heart the universal, moral law of God, and so treated his neighbor as he would like to have been treated.

That is not for the church, that is for the world. That is the old commandment. We have not yet come to the new commandment. This is the commandment God had given in the hearts of men and through the law of Moses—a moral, universal law for everybody. This is the minimum degree of love a person should have. I wonder if we have this minimum? In these days God is renewing His church. Many people think that renewal is to speak in tongues. That's not renewal. Renewal begins when we acknowledge that our hearts are not full of love, that they are, in fact, empty. Renewal comes when our confession brings us to God crying for mercy—and the grace to love as we ought.

We sing, "All one body we, one in hope, and doctrine, one in charity. . . ." That's not true! The problem of the church is not that she has no love. That is *a* problem, but not *the* problem. The problem is that she *has not* love and believes she *has*. If a person is barren and knows it, there is hope. But if a person is barren and doesn't know it, she is in trouble. We sing that we are one, but it's a lie. We are not one, we are divided. Nor are we one in love. We have not yet even come up to the minimum standard of the world.

# CHAPTER 11

# Three Degrees of Love: The New Commandment

There must have been a lot of excitement among Jesus' disciples when he said, "A new commandment I give unto you." They knew only the ten commandments. Now the Lord was giving the eleventh commandment.

"What is it, Lord?"

"That ye love one another."

"We knew that!"

"No, listen, as I have loved you, that ye love one another."

This is another picture, "as I have loved you."

There is a limit to the old commandment. I will love my neighbor insofar as I am not in danger, because I have to love myself too. If I have a bowl of soup, I give him half but also save half for myself. The love of Jesus is much more, because He gave all of Himself for us. He gave His life! The old commandment, to love thy neighbor as thyself, ends here. The new commandment is a love that loves unto death. "Love one another as I have loved you."

How many times does Jesus forgive you every day? One, two, three, four, how many? We cannot measure the love of Jesus for us. This is the same love we must have among ourselves. Jesus came to unite us again, to create a family where sacrificial love maintains the family.

But there is an enormous obstacle that opposes the

expression of this love. It is the basic structure or frame of my life. We want to change the structures of the church. People say, "Let's change Sunday school, let's appoint new officers, let's move. . . ." But no change in outward structures will help unless we change our own internal structures.

Buildings in Argentina, where it is so cold and rainy, are mostly concrete. To build them, the first thing we do is make concrete columns for the frame. Then we add the bricks, the windows, and all the other things that make a building. Alterations on the basic frame are easy. You can put a wall here or there as you like. You can modify it for use as a house, a hospital, or a school, without changing the structure of the building. You buy an old house whose frame is still good and say, "I don't like this window, I'll transform it into a door." You can change the whole house so it looks new. But it is still the same structure underneath.

The same thing happened with many of us. We became evangelicals and we changed walls, but not structures.

One of my friends said to me, "Oh, brother, what a change since I was saved!"

"What happened?" I asked.

"Before I was saved when I fought with my wife, I said bad words to her, we threw things at each other. But praise the Lord, since we are saved, when we fight we don't say bad words any more."

It is the same structure with slight alterations. There are people who used to fight in the taverns. They were saved and have become deacons. Now they fight in the church with the Board of Trustees. Pastors fight at conventions. Churches declare war on one another—all for the sake of "defending the faith." Any Christian who has been a church member for more than a year has learned the basic skills of hand-to-hand fighting in the congregations. Some things have been changed, but the basic structure remains the same.

In *Good News for Modern Man* there is a picture of a woman with a heavy burden. She gets to the cross, leaves her burden there, and continues on, now walking upright. But we are not to leave the burden at the cross. We are to leave ourselves.

The cross is like an atomic bomb that must be placed right in the basement of our building. PLLOOOW! All down! God's plan begins with a program of demolition to make room for a totally new structure built on a new foundation: Christ. I am the great hindrance to love. We need to pass again in front of the cross and say, "Jesus, excuse me. I forgot the most important thing. I left only my burdens, but now I leave myself as well."

Jesus said, "If anyone wants to follow me, he must first deny himself." That is, forget about yourself, take up your cross and follow Him.

What does it mean to take up the cross? One interpretation says the cross is a sickness, another says it's when the mother-in-law lives at home. It's simpler than either of these. When anyone in the Roman Empire saw someone going through the city with a cross on his back, he *knew* what was going to happen. When anybody walked down the streets, "taking his cross," he was due to die shortly. To take up the cross is to say, "Jesus, I'm ready any time." To go with the cross on your shoulder is to have already received the death sentence.

We have an interesting way, however, of avoiding this

commitment to the death that will remove us as the obstacle to love. When Jesus gives us this commandment we endorse it back to Him. He says, "Love!" And we say, "Oh, Lord, *give* me love." Then, if we don't love, He is guilty because He didn't give it to us. But to love is a commandment, and it is one I can keep because I can choose the cross. My failure to love is really the result of my unwillingness to die, not of the Lord's failure to provide. Yes, He gives it. Everything comes from Him. But He commands us to love. He must be the power steering, but we have to move the wheel. He might be the power brake, but we have to press it. He puts the strength in it. But you will die asking for love as long as you regard it as a gift easily bestowed.

One pastor I know likes his people to love one another. When they have communion he says, "Wait! Don't take communion until you are at peace with one another." How blind we are to our own lack of love. I think ministers have an extra problem in this respect because they jealously guard their sheep. Jealousy leaves no room for love in a man's heart. Many times the people long to come together. It's the leaders who don't want to love.

Not long ago we had a healing campaign in Argentina. On the last day the speaker asked all the pastors present to come to the microphone. We went up. Each of us gave his church name, the days they have meetings and so forth. "I am from the Pentecostal church," "I am from the Assembly of God," "I am Plymouth Brethren." When I got to the microphone I thought, "What can I say?" And then it came to me. I said, "I am from the Church for Everybody. . . ." All the people began to clap their hands and shout. I said, "What happened?" I didn't realize it to begin with, but the people liked the name: "The Church for Everybody." The people liked it! But not one of the pastors clapped.

Once fifty-four church leaders from Argentina travelled to Bogota, Colombia, for a big congress. On the plane I said to one of them, "What a problem it would be for the church in Argentina if we should crash with all these leaders!" My friend suggested, "Perhaps that would be the solution!"

Shepherds, *we* have to start to obey the new commandment. What kind of teachers are we that we teach others to do what we haven't even lifted a finger to perform ourselves? That's what the Pharisees did. And Jesus rebuked them. Shepherds in the same city should begin to love one another, even if they can't love men in another city. God has only one church in each city, and we are all shepherds of it. We have to love and to care for one another. If only three, four, or seven pastors began to love one another they could revolutionize their entire city.

"But I have no time; I have this committee, I have that committee. . . ."

I answer, "Brother, these committees are not the first priority. The first priority is what we agree is the most important element of Christian life. If you haven't got that you haven't got anything. We must make time to love. And don't say you lack time. You have the same amount of time that I have. So don't say, 'I have no time.' Tell the truth. Say, 'I have time, but I occupy all my time with myself and my things.'"

Put on your list of first priorities: *love my fellow pastors.* Then put each one's name on this list. Pray for each of them, the Baptist, the Methodist, the Catholic, the one who is with Carl McIntire, the one who is with the World Council of Churches, whoever says he is a minister of God. Today as in New Testament times it is not the publicans and sinners who are far from the kingdom, but the Scribes and Pharisees—the religious people.

In the parable of the wedding feast the host said, "Go and bring in everybody. The good and the bad, and bring them to my house." Why? Because first comes "love." When we were still sinners, Jesus loved us. Love does not ask for prerequisites. If you love, you love the person where you find him. Then after you love, something is going to happen. But first, love.

Some people say, "No, no. First we should speak about doctrine." They are wrong. Love is first. After you love him, it will be so easy. First take away the great beam that is in your eye, and then you'll see to take out that little thing from the eye of that preacher who's with the World Council of Churches.

How do you put this into practice? Let's say I want to establish a relationship with a particular pastor—a pastor who has never been friendly to me. I decide to start next Wednesday. So on Wednesday I am standing at his door . . . knock, knock, knock. . . .

"Hello."

"Ah, good morning, Reverend; ah . . . I am the pastor of the Church for Everybody up on the hill. I have come to visit you."

"Ah, what for?"

"Oh, I just came to . . . visit you."

"Listen, I haven't too much time, you know I am a very busy person. Please tell me why you came."

"I just came to say 'hello' and to find out how your church is doing."

His expression clearly says, "This guy must be crazy."

"Listen, I won't occupy more than five minutes of your time."

"Well, come in."

"How are you, Brother? And how is your church getting along?"

"Quite well. Last Sunday we had a fine meeting, the building was packed. God gave me a very nice sermon."

"Oh, yes? Praise the Lord!"

"And five people came to the altar for prayer. The church is in revival and the finances are going very well."

"Wonderful! And how is your family?"

"My wife is not well right now, but she will be all right."

"Have you any children?"

"Yes, I have three. A boy and two girls."

"How nice. Are they at school?"

"Yes, they are at school; one of them likes to collect stamps and my little girl has a collection of dolls. They do very well in school too."

"Well, Brother, I know you are a very busy person and I have to leave. I'm so glad that I've been to your house. Thank You, Lord, for knowing this brother. Thank You for blessing his wife and children."

After you leave and he closes the door, he'll stand there in the hall and say, "What is the matter with him? I'd better call his superintendent. . . . Hello, are you the superintendent?"

"Yes. . . ."

"Do you know Pastor Ortiz?"

"Yes."

"How is he? Do you think that he is well?"

"Yes, I think he is."

"Well, this morning he came to visit me and he acted strangely. Perhaps he is working too hard. Perhaps you should keep an eye on him, huh? I don't think he is well."

Next week: knock, knock, knock.

"Ah, the crazy one again."

"Hello, Brother, I came to visit you."

"Well, come in" (at least it's short).

"How are you, Brother? How was the meeting last Sunday?"

"We had a nice meeting."

"How is your wife? My wife and I have been praying for her all week. I didn't know if your wife would like to receive visitors. My wife told me she wanted to come, but I said no, you had better not."

"Oh, yes. She could have come."

"I'll tell her. How are your children? I brought these two stamps for your son. I just received them from India. Well, let's pray." I pray and leave.

Next week: knock, knock, knock.

By the the fifth or sixth visit he'll be waiting for you! He'll need that little time of prayer. He'll need your words of love. Don't talk about your church, just try to bless him and find out what he is doing. Love him, love his church and what he is doing. He'll be waiting for you. Then (when he knows it's love) you say, "Brother, come have lunch with us." A friendship will have been born.

Many pastors have said to me, "Well, I tried. But here

in San Jose the pastors don't want to unite. I invited them to a meeting and nobody came . . . then I tried again and still nobody came."

No wonder. Pastors are fed up with meetings. Jesus didn't say, "Invite them to meetings." He said, "Love them." We are pretentious. We don't want to give ourselves. We just want to have impersonal official things. Give your house, your wife, your children, your money; give yourself for the pastor—not a meeting! A meeting is nothing. If the meeting starts at eight, he comes one minute to eight. He says hello and sits for an hour looking at the back of another man's neck. Any words exchanged are just words of politeness. That's not communion.

Pastors are lonely people who need love. Many pastors fall into sin because they are alone. There's no communion, no family. And when a pastor falls into sin, much of the guilt lies on the other pastors.

Invite him to play golf, or to have ice cream with you. He may be anti-charismatic, but no pastor is anti-ice cream, and very few are anti-golf. After you play golf with him, after you serve him ice cream, invite him to your house. He will probably invite you to his house after that. You become friends. Now is the time to share your theological concerns with him. You can discuss anything with a person who loves you.

We must have one church in each city, and we *will* have it if pastors get together.

Is this too hard? What I have described is much less than giving your life. God wants more. God wants you to give everything you have for one loving church. This, then, is something that must start with the shepherds.

I once had an enemy. He said, "You are not faithful

to our denomination." Eventually he started to hate me. At one of the conventions, I went up and said, "Hello, how are you?" and I hugged him.

He said, "Don't hug me! I don't love you!"

"I love you, Brother," I said.

"You cannot love me because I am your enemy."

I replied, "Praise the Lord, I know you are my enemy. But this is an opportunity to love my enemy. Thank You, Jesus, for my enemy. Bless you, enemy!" One year later I was preaching in his church. Love is the most powerful weapon we have.

A boy meets a young lady in the snack bar at the university. The next day he calls her on the phone.

"Hello?"

"Mary, this is Pablo. You remember meeting me yesterday? Please come by tomorrow at eight. We're going to get married."

She doesn't go. First there must be friendship, then a courtship. He must take time to conquer her emotions through love. How will a pastor get "married" with other pastors if he doesn't conquer them first? So the chain starts. Love must start among the shepherds.

Praise the Lord, a new day is coming. In almost every capital city of Latin America, the pastors are coming together. God is starting to awaken the spiritual harmony of love. What shall you do when it comes to the United States? Will you shut the door? Will you be left out?

How did Jesus love you? He gave His life. We all know John 3:16, but do we know the other John 3:16, 1 John 3:16? "Hereby perceive we the love of God, because he laid down his life for us: and we ought to lay down our lives for the brethren." Do we understand what it means to lay down our lives for the brethren? This is the same kind of love that Jesus demands from us for each other—the kind He had for us.

I have people in my life, apart from my wife and children, for whom I would give my life. And I know people who would give their lives for me.

A friend told me not long ago, "Juan Carlos, I told Jesus that if He needs even my life to save yours, it's His." I know a Catholic priest who loves me so much he would give his life for me! This is the kind of love God wants us to have within the family of God. "Jesus in us" means loving in His manner, through us.

The "old commandment" love said, "Love your neighbor as yourself." It was a love with limits, a love that included our love for ourselves. It meant I would love my neighbor unless it endangered me.

But now we are entering into "new commandment" love. The old commandment called for a minimum of love. Yet often we think even that is too much because we don't have love at all. We speak of the minimum and think we are speaking of the maximum. The old commandment applies to neighbors. But in the church we are part of a family. New commandment love is for the church, where my neighbor becomes my brother.

Something is starting to happen. God is going to have a new community. The world has not witnessed what a church is yet. But the world will know what this new community, this light of the world will be. We are going to be like a city, an exemplary community, whose members love one another.

# CHAPTER 12

# Three Degrees of Love: Perfect Union

The minimum degree of love, old commandment love, is to love your neighbor as yourself. New commandment love is to lay down your life for the brethren. The final degree of love is found in John 17:26. "Father, I have made thy name known to them and will make it known, that the love wherewith thou hast loved me may be in them, and I in them." This is the love of the Trinity.

How the Father loves the Son. How the Son loves the Father. How the Spirit loves the Son. How the Spirit loves the Father. How the Father loves the Spirit. How the Son loves the Spirit. Can you imagine that love? It is an eternal perfect love in that it assures we will never be in disagreement.

In the Old Testament the Father did miracles and wonders. He raised the dead and healed the sick. Then the Son came. He did the same thing, yet the Father was not jealous. The Father was glad. Then the Son departed and the Holy Spirit arrived. He, too, is raising the dead and healing the sick. Still there is no fighting among them because the three are doing the same thing. They never fight. Why? Because they love one another. They never get offended at anything.

Trinity love is the love that makes the three to be one.

Two plus eternal love equals one. A hundred plus eternal love equals one. This is the love that transforms an entire group of people into one: Trinity love, one in the other.

When I was a Sunday school kid, I once heard the teacher say that we were "in" Christ. I understood that. The next Sunday, however, he taught that Christ was "in us." I objected. "Teacher, you are wrong. Last Sunday you said we were in Christ. Now you say He is in us. How can that be? If He is in us, we cannot be in Him at the same time. One must be in the other, it cannot be both things at the same time."

I didn't understand because I was so far removed from that kind of love. Now it is easy to understand. If I am in my brother's heart and he in mine, then we are one.

Of course to begin with we are not one. We are many. It is this love that makes us one.

When we start to love one another, the word "brother" is going to disappear from our conversation. We call one another "brother," but we don't live as brothers. If we lived as brothers, we wouldn't call each other "brother." I was called "Skinny" in my home as a boy. My brothers did not call me "Brother Juan Carlos." They called me "Skinny," because I was a brother. We say "Pastor," "Reverend," and "Brother" to people with whom we have only formal relationships. Those titles show that we are without love for one another. When I call Pete Lopez "brother" it is because we are not brothers, but we want it to appear that we are brothers.

I was scandalized once when I went to another church and the pastor called on a member in his congregation. "Mister Brown, will you lead us in prayer?" How worldly these people are, I thought. They say "mister" but in our church we say "brother." Yet when I studied the difference between that church and mine, the relationship among the "misters" was the same as we had among the "brothers." We were fooling ourselves with words.

Not long ago we had a four-hour meeting in our church celebrating the Lord's Supper. How can you stretch the Lord's Supper out so long, you ask? Well, we bought twenty pounds of bread—the Bible does not tell us how much bread the disciples ate—and gave a whole loaf to each group of four people. Then we started breaking the bread and eating. As this was happening we all began to hug and kiss. Then one would ask another, "What are your needs?" And after a while the money began flying all over the place. Four hours of the Lord's Supper—with love.

The Holy Spirit is doing a new thing among the people of God. He is regrouping them. What do I mean by regrouping? Up to now we were grouped by denomination, race, age, sex, and the like. We were Methodist, Pentecostal, Presbyterian, Holiness, Nazarene, Roman Catholic, Salvation Army, Episcopalian, Plymouth Brethren, Baptist. Now He is grouping into two categories only: those who love one another and those who don't. He is doing it not by our doctrine, but by the way we live together and love one another!

The sheep and the goats are the only two groups God knows. There are plenty of sheep in Argentina. They always huddle close, with their heads together, like one body. And there are plenty of goats. The goats have their backs to each other, bucking and kicking. You don't need the gift of discernment to know who is a sheep and who is a goat.

Jesus wants us to be one. Just as the Trinity is one—Father, Son, and Holy Spirit—so he wants us to be one. He wants this not only in evangelistic efforts and in fellowship meetings; He wants us to love one another as a family in every city in every country.

We Christians are like potatoes. After the seed potato is put into the ground, the potatoes grow as tubers, three or four to each plant. They are together but lack unity. At harvest time the potatoes are dug up and placed in the same sack. Still, this is not unity, it is merely regrouping. It is confraternity, it is fellowship, but not unity.

Later when the potatoes are peeled and put together, they tell each other, "Now we are one." No, not yet. They must be cut and cooked together because what God wants is mashed potatoes.

So now there are many potatoes, but they are destined to become one bowlful of mashed potatoes. And when the potatoes are mashed, no single potato can say, "Look at me. I am bigger than you."

That is what the Holy Spirit wants and He is starting to do it throughout the world. He is renewing His church with love. He is telling us, "Let's love one another with all our hearts." This is the key for evangelization. Jesus prayed "that they may be one," and that prayer will be answered.

Hallelujah!

*For a free copy of*

**LOGOS JOURNAL**

*send your name and address to*

Logos Journal

Box 191

Plainfield, New Jersey 07060

*and say, "one free Journal, please."*